nk
6.30

RHETORIC AS A
DRAMATIC LANGUAGE
IN BEN JONSON

Rhetoric as a Dramatic Language in Ben Jonson

By ALEXANDER H. SACKTON

1967
OCTAGON BOOKS, INC.
New York

Reprinted 1967

by special arrangement with Columbia University Press

OCTAGON BOOKS, INC.
175 FIFTH AVENUE
NEW YORK, N. Y. 10010

LIBRARY OF CONGRESS CATALOG CARD NUMBER: 67-18783

Printed in U.S.A. by
NOBLE OFFSET PRINTERS, INC.
NEW YORK 3, N. Y.

TO MY FATHER

They are the Noblest benefits, and sinke
Deepest in Man, of which when he doth thinke,
The memorie delights him more, from whom
Than what he hath receiv'd.

PREFACE

THIS STUDY attempts to describe in detail certain values which Jonson created with rhetoric. In his plays rhetoric becomes a dramatic language through which he communicates indirectly with his audience. I have chosen jargon and the language of hyperbole for special analysis because they are prominent and recognized characteristics of Jonson's style, and representative forms of language to which Jonson gave a distinct rhetorical aim.

To Professor Douglas Bush, for his patient reading of the chapters as they were first written, I owe a debt that cannot be estimated. I am happy to recall conversations with him on the questions which they raised. His criticism was invaluable to me in revision. I wish to thank also Professor Harry Levin for reading the manuscript in an earlier form, and Professors Theodore Spencer and F. O. Matthiessen for the encouragement they gave me at the beginning of this study.

The publishers of the following works have kindly given permission to quote copyright material: *The Works of Chaucer*, edited by F. N. Robinson, Houghton, Mifflin Company, Boston; Horace, *Satires, Epistles and Ars Poetica*, translated by H. R. Fairclough, Loeb Classical Library, Harvard University Press, Cambridge, Mass.; *Ben Jonson*, edited by C. H. Herford, Percy and Evelyn Simpson, *The Works of Thomas Kyd*, edited by F. S. Boas, *The Works of John Lyly*, edited by R. W. Bond, Oxford University Press, Oxford; Christopher Marlowe, *Tamburlaine the Great*, edited by U. M. Ellis-Fermor, *The Jew of Malta*, edited by H. S. Bennett, Methuen and Company Ltd., London; John Marston, *The Scourge of Villainie*, edited by G. B. Harrison, E. P. Dutton and Company, New York; *The Plays of John Marston,* edited by H. Harvey Wood, Oliver and Boyd, Ltd., Edinburgh; *The Complete Works of Shakespeare,* edited by George Lyman Kittredge, Ginn and Company, Boston.

ALEXANDER H. SACKTON

Austin, Texas
February, 1948

CONTENTS

RHETORIC AS A
DRAMATIC LANGUAGE
IN BEN JONSON

By wordes the wise thou shalt espye,
By wordes a foole sone shalt thou trye.

Tottel's Miscellany

Could these brave prancing words with action's spur,
Be ridden thoroughly, and managed right
'Twould fright the audience, and perhaps delight.

CHAPMAN, The Gentleman Usher

CHAPTER I

APPROACH TO BEN JONSON

"'TIS OBSERVABLE," James Upton pointed out in 1749, commenting on the Prologue to *Volpone*, "that Jonson calls himself here a *poet*, and his plays, *poems;* making use of expressions importing dignity and honour." [1] Since Upton wrote, Jonson's reputation as a dramatic poet has suffered much, but today the current estimate of his plays as dramatic poems is being reexamined. Like Dryden, and others who inherited the tradition which he represented in the preceding age, Jonson stands to profit by the revolution in taste which calls in question many assumptions of Romantic criticism. At least he is getting a new hearing. The emotional tone of his characteristic work is no longer considered inimical to poetry. The deliberateness with which he wrote is not necessarily uninspired, nor his use of a literary tradition necessarily uncreative. The fact that he was a great critic does not preclude him from being a great poet also. These are the assumptions of the more independent modern criticism of Jonson. [2] The older point of view, which is not unknown today, goes back to the eighteenth century, [3] and became firmly established in the nineteenth. Its most general weakness is that it fails to treat Jonson's plays as dramatic poems. Component parts or aspects of a play are considered with little regard to their dramatic value or their relation to the whole. A play is treated as if it were "a study in vulgar realism" or a study of various types of characters. [4] Characters are analyzed and dis-

---

[1] *Remarks on Three Plays of Benjamin Jonson* (London, 1749), p. 2.

[2] T. S. Eliot, *Selected Essays* (London, 1932), pp. 147–60; L. C. Knights, *Drama and Society in the Age of Jonson* (London, 1937), pp. 179–227; Harry Levin, *Ben Jonson Selected Works* (New York, 1938), "Introduction."

[3] Its development may be observed in Robert Gale Noyes, *Ben Jonson on the English Stage 1660–1776* (Cambridge, Mass., 1935).

[4] G. Gregory Smith, *Ben Jonson* (London, 1919), pp. 116–17.

cussed as creatures independent of their context, not as a medium of dramatic expression. If they are identified with the supposed object of Jonson's satiric attack, the reading is further narrowed. Some of the early plays are treated as if Jonson wrote them only to attack his personal enemies,[5] while a play like *The Alchemist* is considered an attack upon "a specific class of sharpers." [6] Such an insistence on a narrow literal meaning is due to the failure to read the play as a work of literature. Other than literary interests have been common among Jonson's readers. Antiquarians and historians have found him useful. The interest of his personality, the comparatively full knowledge we have of him from sources outside of his work, and the number of pronouncements which he himself made on his aims, have cast a shadow over his work and have made it difficult to concentrate attention upon his plays as plays.

However, it is now becoming a commonplace of criticism that an Elizabethan play may be approached most profitably, not as a study in human character, or as an expression of an individual philosophy, but as a dramatic poem. Such an approach involves in the first place a study of language, the medium in which a play is given form. The traditional criticism has treated language like other constituent elements of a dramatic composition. Its learned content, which is perhaps its most obvious characteristic in Jonson, is studied without reference to its dramatic use. Gregory Smith considers it one of the "inconveniences" of Jonson's style, although he recognizes its dramatic value in the speech of Epicure Mammon.[7] Other qualities are admired or condemned without regard to their dramatic value. Both Lamb and Hazlitt characteristically praise the "poetry" of some of

[5] Oscar James Campbell points out how this preoccupation has inhibited the appreciation of *Poetaster* as a play (*Comicall Satyre and Shakespeare's Troilus and Cressida*, San Marino, Calif., 1938, pp. 109–10).

[6] Felix E. Schelling, *Elizabethan Drama 1558–1642* (2 vols., Boston and New York, 1908), I, 531.

[7] *Ben Jonson*, p. 115. Herford and Simpson express a more sympathetic view of Jonson's learning: in "style and diction," they write, "the scholar and

the least dramatic speeches in the Jonsonian canon.[8] When Lamb praises the speeches of Epicure Mammon, he does so without reference to their dramatic context.[9] Even Coleridge, although he makes valuable observations elsewhere on Jonson's plays, condemns a speech of Sejanus as "absurd rant and *ventriloquism*," without considering its relation to its context.[10] Poetry and drama are in fact impossible to separate in a dramatic poem. The two values are interdependent, parts of one whole,[11] and the medium in which they are united is language.

Although the dramatic values of Jonson's language have been neglected, scattered observations upon its general character have not been uncommon.[12] Gregory Smith observes that Jonson "had always the artist's sense and care of language," and that he "tasted words and phrases as a connoisseur," [13] but, in the absence of detailed application, such statements are not

---

the dramatist co-operated to admirable purpose" (*Ben Jonson*, ed. C. H. Herford, Percy and Evelyn Simpson, 10 vols., Oxford, 1925- , I, 124).

[8] Hazlitt writes: "Two of the most poetical passages in Ben Jonson, are the description of Echo in Cynthia's Revels, and the fine comparison of the mind to a temple in the New Inn; a play which, on the whole, however, I can read with no patience" (*Lectures on the Dramatic Literature of the Age of Elizabeth*, in *The Collected Works of William Hazlitt*, ed. A. R. Waller and Arnold Glover, 13 vols., London and New York, 1902-6, V, 265). In his *Specimens of English Dramatic Poets* (in *Works*, ed. William MacDonald, 12 vols., London, 1903, I, 168-71), Lamb quotes a "Beautiful" but undramatic passage from *The New Inn* to illustrate Jonson's "poetical fancy."

[9] *Works*, I, 161.

[10] *Coleridge's Miscellaneous Criticism*, ed. Thomas Middleton Raysor (London, 1936), p. 54.

[11] M. C. Bradbrook writes: "The essential structure of Elizabethan drama lies not in the narrative or the characters but in the words. The greatest poets are also the greatest dramatists. Through their unique interest in word play and word patterns of all kinds the Elizabethans were especially fitted to build their drama on words" (*Themes and Conventions of Elizabethan Tragedy*, Cambridge, England, 1935, p. 5).

[12] Different non-dramatic aspects of Jonson's language are studied by Joshua H. Neumann, "Notes on Ben Jonson's English," *PMLA*, LIV (1939), 736-63, and Frederic I. Carpenter, *Metaphor and Simile* (Chicago, 1895), pp. 127-56.

[13] *Ben Jonson*, p. 269.

helpful to a reader of Jonson. Some more specific qualities of Jonson's language were pointed out by a critic in the early stages of Romantic criticism: "Though his comic characters do not actually wear the buskin," Charles Dibdin wrote, "yet the sock has such high heels and is made of such stiff materials, that the characters stalk instead of trip, and thus we have quaintness for nature, affectation for grace, and awkwardness for ease."[14] The many admiring readers of Jonson who expressed themselves in the seventeenth century frequently commend his language, sometimes for the very quality which Dibdin deplores. It was a positive virtue to Robert Mead that Jonson

> . . . grovels not in's *Satires*, but soares high,
> Strikes at the mounting *vices* . . .[15]

Jasper Mayne also praises the elevated language of Jonson's plays:

> . . . thy *language* and thy *stile* so high,
> Thy *Socke* to th' *ancle*, *Buskin* reacht to th' *thigh*.[16]

It was commonly repeated in the seventeenth century that Jonson "made our Language pure and good,"[17] though Dryden made some strictures on his use of Latin idiom and on the qualities of wit which "*are extremely wanting in* Ben. Johnson."[18] But although these nearly contemporary readers of Jonson made some suggestive observations on Jonson's plays, and Dryden made a critical examen of *The Silent Woman*, the treatment of language is general and not applied to a specific play or dramatic situation. One cannot expect modern critical terms in seventeenth-century criticism, but some idea of the kind of pleasure readers then got from Jonson is suggested by

---

[14] *A Complete History of the English Stage*, 5 vols. (London, 1800), III, 296; quoted by Noyes, *Ben Jonson on the English Stage*, p. 169.

[15] *Jonsonus Virbius* (London, 1638), p. 59; reprinted by Jesse F. Bradley and Joseph Quincy Adams, *The Jonson Allusion-Book* (New Haven, 1922), p. 245.

[16] *Jonsonus Virbius*, p. 31 (*Jonson Allusion-Book*, p. 227).

[17] John Beaumont in *Jonsonus Virbius*, p. 12 (*Jonson Allusion-Book*, p. 212).

[18] "Preface" to *An Evening's Love*, in *The Dramatic Works* ed. Montague Summers (6 vols., London, 1931), II, 243.

the emphasis on the need for studying him. "*Thou* exact'st our best houres industrie," Richard West wrote; we may "read" Shakespeare and Beaumont, "we ought to study thee." [19] Thomas Fuller observed that Jonson's comedies "took not so well at the first stroke as at the rebound, when beheld the second time; yea, they will endure reading." [20] The reward of close study of Jonson's plays, and more particularly of his language, is suggested by Coleridge's experience. "The more I study his writings," Coleridge wrote, "the more I admire them; and the more the study resembles that of an ancient classic, in the *minutiæ* of his rhythm, metre, choice of words, forms of connection, etc., the more numerous have the points of admiration become." [21] Jonson labored to produce his art, and "things, wrote with labour," he said, "deserve to be so read." [22]

This labor of reading, if it is to elucidate his art, is not to be spent in tracking down Jonson's learning, but in a close examination of his language, and the study of its place in a dramatic context. Coleridge recognized the injustice of much Jonsonian criticism when he insisted that Jonson wrote an "altogether different *genus* of the drama" [23] from Shakespeare's. He cannot therefore be understood properly, if he is judged by the same standards. Shakespeare's language as a dramatic medium has been studied with interesting results by observing its recurrent themes in imagery, as if it were a musical composition. Such an approach to Jonson's language might tell us something about Jonson's interests, as Caroline Spurgeon has shown, [24] but it would hardly throw light on the art of his plays. The first problem which faces the critic who proposes to study Jonson's plays as dramatic poems is to determine what kind of linguistic approach is likely to elucidate them. An approach to Jonson

[19] *Jonsonus Virbius*, p. 56 (*Jonson Allusion-Book*, p. 243).
[20] *The History of the Worthies of England*, ed. P. Austin Nuttall (3 vols., London, 1840), II, 425.
[21] *Coleridge's Miscellaneous Criticism*, p. 49.
[22] *Discoveries*, in *Ben Jonson*, ed. Herford and Simpson, VIII, 638.
[23] *Coleridge's Miscellaneous Criticism*, p. 57.
[24] *Shakespeare's Imagery* (New York, 1936), especially Chart IV.

through his language seems peculiarly relevant. A casual reader of his plays is impressed by the number of references to language itself. Jonson is not unlike other Elizabethans in this respect, but in the frequency and dramatic importance of such references, he is probably unique. His *dramatis personae* are often conscious of their own language, or they comment on the language of other characters. Even in the absence of comment the audience is sometimes expected to be aware not only of what is said but of the language employed in saying it, which is often more important. Elizabethans studied as the art of rhetoric the use of such language. In Jonson's plays it may be the language of persuasion by which knaves dupe their victims, or it may be a formal speech of praise or description, the dramatic effect of which depends upon the rhetorical quality of its style. This elevated character of language, in comedy as well as tragedy, has long been recognized by Jonson's readers and critics,[25] but its dramatic effects have never been a subject of study. Although rhetorical expression is often superficial, it is the very superficiality that Jonson uses for dramatic effect. Coleridge observed that Jonson "was a very accurately observing man; but he cared only to observe what was external or open to, and likely to impress, the senses." [26] T. S. Eliot seems to have observed the result in Jonson's poetry when he said "his poetry is of the surface"; it deals "with the surface of life." [27] In dealing with the surface of life, Jonson dealt with "what was external or open to, and likely to impress, the senses," that is, the world of appearance. The language of this world is the language of rhetoric. Rhetoric,

[25] Passing references are especially common in John Addington Symonds, *Ben Jonson* (New York, 1886); it is characteristically treated not as a dramatic phenomenon, but as a part of a realistic representation of character. "Sir Epicure Mammon exhibits in his rhetoric the calenture of a brain inflamed by the expectation of absolutely illimitable power over nature" (p. 105. See also pp. 59, 169). E. E. Stoll, in defending Jonson against William Archer, says, "There is in him no high-flying rhetoric except by way of burlesque or satire" (*Poets and Playwrights*, Minneapolis, 1930, p. 148). The exceptions, however, are too numerous and too important to be dismissed with such general terms as "burlesque or satire."

[26] *Coleridge's Miscellaneous Criticism*, p. 46.   [27] *Selected Essays*, p. 148.

used rather to impress the hearer than to express genuine or
deep feeling, is the language of appearance. Words in Jonson,
as Harry Levin has observed, are frequently used for their own
sake. What is said often does not matter. In *Epicoene*, for example, "everything spoken has a high nuisance value and words
themselves become sheer filigree." [28] This formal quality of
Jonson's language is part of his technique of communication.
Though the words themselves may be practically without
meaning, they acquire new meaning from a dramatic context.
They also form larger patterns of an episode or a character, and
these in turn are parts of a still larger pattern. One recalls the
sets of balanced male and female characters in *Cynthia's Revels*,
and the introduction in single file of the characters of *Volpone*. The study of rhetoric in Jonson's plays may therefore
provide the appropriate linguistic approach which we are seeking. Its relevance will be tested in the following chapters.

The dramatic meaning which subsists beneath the rhetoric
of Jonson's drama could be appreciated most by a sophisticated
audience. In many references to his audience scattered throughout his writings, Jonson makes quite clear that he was addressing the educated and the thoughtful. His earliest admirers who
express themselves point out frequently his appeal to the judgment. Jasper Mayne was pleased to observe that his "*Stage* was
still a *Stage*," and the audience was not asked fancifully to accept
"two entrances" as "two *parts* o' the *world*, disjoin'd by
Seas." [29] Jonson's audience was expected to be constantly vigi-
lant in exercising a critical judgment on the speech and actions
of his dramatic characters. It is therefore not difficult to understand why his plays were most popular among the more educated classes, nor why his reputation suffered in the latter part
of the eighteenth century. A writer in 1771 complains of "an
unimpassioned coldness in the Language" of *Every Man in His
Humor*, and contends that "it is easier to write to the judgment,

[28] *Ben Jonson Selected Works*, p. 30.
[29] *Jonsonus Virbius*, p. 31 (*Jonson Allusion-Book*, p. 227).

than to the feelings of the heart." [30] It is also easier to indulge the feelings of the heart than to discipline oneself to the rigors of Jonsonian feeling.

The kind of education which Jonson assumed in his audience was not specialized, for the study of language was central in the Renaissance ideal of liberal training. Rhetoric meant so much more to the Renaissance than it means today that it seems necessary to describe its older significance in some detail. It represents a training which Jonson shared to a certain extent with his audience. Lawyers, preachers, courtiers, and diplomats were as familiar with it as poets and playwrights, and the interest in the ways of using language among these classes filtered down to the unlettered classes which imitated them.

[30] *The Public Ledger,* November 12, 1771; quoted by Noyes, *Ben Jonson on the English Stage,* p. 287.

CHAPTER II

THE TRADITION OF RHETORIC IN THE AGE OF JONSON

A LIVELY INTEREST in words and their use was common among Elizabethan theatergoers; this interest had been fostered and developed in the tradition of rhetorical education; and Elizabethan writers were themselves conscious of the rhetorical principles of composition. These premises hardly need to be proved, since they are widely accepted. Besides, Jonson makes abundantly clear the presence of rhetorical speech in his plays, and its effect on a modern reader is not dependent wholly upon a knowledge of the Elizabethan background. The modern conception of rhetoric being what it is, however, it seems desirable to indicate the nature and importance of rhetorical study in England during the Renaissance, and the kind of interest in language which it fostered.

One of the numerous medieval traditions which flourished with new vigor in the Renaissance is the study of rhetoric. The early Christians, though hostile at first to all forms of pagan culture, inevitably succumbed to the influence of classical rhetoric [1] after Christianity became the official religion of the Empire. Many of the Christian fathers of the fourth century were trained in the sophistic tradition,[2] and applied their secular learning in the service of the church. Before his conversion, Augustine had been a teacher of rhetoric, and in the principles

[1] Gaston Boissier, *La Fin du paganisme*, 2d ed., 2 vols. (Paris, 1894), I, 199–218.

[2] See Thomas E. Ameringer, *The Stylistic Influence of the Second Sophistic on the Panegyrical Sermons of St. John Chrysostom* (Washington, 1921), pp. 20–28; James M. Campbell, *The Influence of the Second Sophistic on the Style of the Sermons of St. Basil the Great* (Washington, 1922), pp. 14–19; Louis Méridier, *L'Influence de la seconde sophistique sur l'œuvre de Grégoire de Nysse* (Paris, 1906), pp. 53–69.

which he lays down in *De Doctrina Christiana*, he recalls the study to its ancient purpose, as Aristotle and Cicero understood it, to make the truth prevail.[3] Such an art deserved a place in the education of a Christian priest. The Roman system of education, in which rhetoric was emphasized, could therefore be justified for Christians. In this early period, rhetoric received greater attention than either grammar or logic, although the primary emphasis changed in the later Middle Ages, first to grammar, then to logic.[4] But the art which had been born and had flourished under democratic forms of government was limited in its scope in the Middle Ages. Although *De oratore* and *Institutio oratoria* were known to men like John of Salisbury,[5] the tradition was most generally represented by Cicero's *De inventione* and the pseudo-Ciceronian *Rhetorica ad Herennium*.[6] Medieval treatments of rhetoric, which were generally addressed to literary craftsmen, almost invariably follow the latter work in the classification of tropes and figures.[7] The traditional five parts of rhetoric were known, but the greatest emphasis was placed upon *elocutio*, which meant stylistic ornament. *Dispositio* was not entirely neglected, but it was reduced to enumerating the different ways of beginning and ending a composition.[8] The places of *inventio* receive extensive treatment in the discussions of am-

[3] *De Doctrina Christiana*, bk. iv, chap. 28, tr. J. F. Shaw (in *The Works of Aurelius Augustine*, ed. Marcus Dods, 3d ed., 15 vols., Edinburgh, 1883, IX, 168–69).

[4] Stephen d'Irsay, *Histoire des universités* (2 vols., Paris, 1933–35), I, 32–38; Charles Sears Baldwin, *Medieval Rhetoric and Poetic* (New York, 1928), p. 151.

[5] *De oratore* was among the MSS which he bequeathed to the library at Chartres, where he had been a student. The famous school there used methods recommended by Quintilian, with whom John shows some familiarity (J. E. Sandys, *History of Classical Scholarship*, 2d ed., Cambridge, England, 1906, pp. 539–41).

[6] These were the textbooks used at the famous University of Bologna (Hastings Rashdall, *The Universities of Europe in the Middle Ages*, ed. F. M. Powicke and A. B. Emden, 3 vols., Oxford, 1936, I, 248).

[7] Edmond Faral, *Les Arts poétiques du xiie et du xiiie siècle* (Paris, 1924), pp. 49–51.

[8] *Ibid.*, p. 55.

plification, which comes to mean simply dilating or developing.[9] Because of the political conditions prevailing in Italy, and the strength of classical tradition, rhetoric received its greatest attention in the south, especially at the University of Bologna.[10] It was there in the eleventh century that the practical *ars dictaminis* was developed, and elementary legal studies were made a part of rhetorical training.[11] The art of the *dictamen* became important in other medieval universities, and sometimes represented the whole field of rhetoric.[12] It attempted only to train writers of letters and official documents, but these were often elaborately conventional and did not represent an ordinary accomplishment. Rhetorical theory was also applied to the formal art of preaching, and when sermons became increasingly popular in the thirteenth century, there were written, especially in England, many tracts in which methods of dilating and dividing the sermon were emphasized.[13]

This attention to the art of writing during the Middle Ages, and its relation to the rhetorical tradition, indicate that the interest in rhetoric was not a new thing in the Renaissance. The text of *Rhetorica ad Herennium* continued to be important [14] even after the mature works of Cicero and the *Institutio* of Quintilian became widely and completely known.[15] The emphasis on practical formulae in the books of the Renaissance

[9] *Ibid.,* p. 61.   [10] Rashdall, *The Universities of Europe,* I, 92–93.   [11] *Ibid.*
[12] Louis J. Paetow, "The Arts Course at Medieval Universities" (*University of Illinois, The University Studies,* Vol. III, No. 7, Urbana, 1910), p. 70.
[13] G. R. Owst, *Preaching in Medieval England* (Cambridge, England, 1926), pp. 314–16.
[14] Thomas Wilson for his *Arte of Rhetorique* uses it as well as the works of Cicero and Quintilian (Russell H. Wagner, "Wilson and His Sources," *Quarterly Journal of Speech,* XV, 1929, 530).
[15] Poggio discovered the complete text of Quintilian in 1416, and in 1422 the principal works of Cicero on rhetoric came to light at Lodi (Charles Sears Baldwin, *Renaissance Literary Theory and Practice,* New York, 1939, p. 44). Aristotle's *Rhetoric* also, which was scarcely known in western Europe during the Middle Ages, became more widely known and in the original Greek. (Marvin T. Herrick, "Early History of Aristotle's *Rhetoric* in England," *Philological Quarterly,* V, 1926, 242–57.)

has more in common with the medieval treatment of rhetoric than with either Cicero or Quintilian. Like the Middle Ages the Renaissance emphasized *elocutio*, and many theorists even excluded *inventio* and *dispositio* from the field of rhetoric. As in the Middle Ages, so also in the Renaissance, rhetorical theory greatly influenced poetic theory. Philosophically, however, the Renaissance, probably under the influence of the newly discovered classical texts, attached more importance to the subject of rhetoric than the Middle Ages had done. The argument of Cicero about the divine attribute of the orator who could rule men's minds, and that of Quintilian about the great civilizing influence of oratory in the history of the race both became current again. Rhetorical study was even extended to include behavior, for the orator, by Cicero's definition, was first of all a good man.

With these new ideas in the air, Renaissance scholars felt that their interest in rhetoric was rather a break with the medieval tradition than a development of it.[16] Rhetoric was closely related to two important and characteristic ideals of the Renaissance: the ideal of the gentleman, and that of public service. Both owe a great deal to the rhetorical tradition, especially to the writings of Cicero, and both in turn are responsible for the increased attention to the art of rhetoric. The Renaissance ideal of the gentleman had its origin in Italy, where the training given to members of the governing class was first made to include letters and the study of ancient culture.[17] It was formed by combining the chivalric ideal of the Middle Ages with the new ideals of learning. The learning of the Renaissance gentleman-scholar, unlike the learning of the medieval clerk, was "polite," based

[16] The number of works on rhetoric and related topics which were published in England in the sixteenth century is an indication of the widespread interest in the subject and of its influence. See J. F. McGrew, "A Bibliography of the Works on Speech Composition in England during the 16th and 17th Centuries," *Quarterly Journal of Speech*, XV (1929), 381–412.

[17] W. H. Woodward, *Studies in Education during the Age of the Renaissance* (Cambridge, England, 1906), p. 246.

upon *litterae humaniores*. Like Cicero's Orator, the gentleman was never to aim at specialization, or become learned in the technical sense, but was to be well enough informed to be conversant on most topics commonly encountered. Most important was the power to use his knowledge effectively in speech. *Il Cortegiano* presents an authoritative picture of the ideal gentleman; more than any other single book it brought the new ideal to northern Europe and to England. The perfect courtier, Castiglione wrote, must "understande how to beehave himself readilye in all occurrentes to drive into his Princis heade what honour and profit shall ensue to him and to his by justice, liberalitie, valiauntnesse of courage, meekenesse and by the other vertues that beelong to a good Prince, and contrariwise what sclaunder and damage commeth of the vices contrarie to them." The fruit of courtliness is "the traininge and the helping forward of the Prince to goodnesse and the fearinge him from yvell." [18] The courtier's education must, therefore, include moral philosophy and the study of eloquence. Although he is not trained especially as a public speaker, he must be, like the ideal orator of tradition, a good man able to teach, delight, and move his audience.

In England the distrust of learning among the governing classes was slow in dying. Early in the sixteenth century, Englishmen made no distinction between polite learning and technical learning. Sir Thomas Elyot observed in 1531 that there were many who "without shame, dare affirme, that to a great gentilman it is a notable reproache to be well lerned and to be called a great clerke." [19] In the eighties both Pettie and Puttenham take account of this persistent feeling. Pettie argued that it was learning "which maketh you gentle men," and by learning, it appears, he meant polite learning:

[18] Baldassare Castiglione, *The Courtier*, tr. Thomas Hoby, 1561 (The Tudor Translations, London, 1900), p. 298.
[19] Sir Thomas Elyot, *The Governour*, 1531 (Everyman's Library, 1907), p. 49.

*Alas you wyll be but ungentle Gentlemen, yf you be no Schollers:
you wyll doo your Prince but simple service, you wyll stande
your Countrey but in slender steade, you wyll bryng your selves
but to small preferment, yf you be no Schollers. Can you coun-
sayle your Prince wysely, foresee daungers providently, governe
matters of state discreetely, without Learning? . . . To come
lower, can you discourse with Strangers, inquire the state of
forraine Countries, geve entertainement to Ambassadours, being
no Schollers? . . . To come lowest of all, Can you so much as
tell your Mistresse a fine tale, or delight her with pleasant device,
beyng unlearned?* [20]

Learning of this kind was precisely that which rhetorical education aimed to teach. Breadth of knowledge and the art of
discourse are required of both the Renaissance gentleman [21] and
Cicero's Orator. Polite learning can only serve its purpose if it is
accompanied by the power of expression. The character of the
ideal gentleman was incomplete if inward feeling was not perfectly reflected in outward action, including speech. Humane
wisdom, ideally at least, had to find its outward expression, and
it could only be in eloquence. The study of philosophy was not
an end in itself; a life of action was the final aim. Euphues is only
being practical when he says the gentleman should "be in-
structed in philosophy, whereby he may attain learning, and
have in all sciences a smack, whereby he may readily dispute of
anything." [22]

This ideal of the gentleman merges into the second ideal
which was fostered by the study of Cicero, and in turn increased
the study of his works on oratory. On the practical side, which
was greatly emphasized, the aim of education, both to Italian
and northern humanists, was to train gentlemen for public

[20] "Preface to the Readers" of *The Civile Conversation of M. Steeven
Guazzo*, the first three books translated by George Pettie, 1581 (The Tudor
Translations, 2 vols., London and New York, 1925), I, 8.

[21] Castiglione would have the courtier learned especially in "those studyes,
which they call Humanitie" (*The Courtier*, pp. 84–85).

[22] John Lyly, *Euphues: the Anatomy of Wit*, 1578 (ed. Morris W. Croll and
Harry Clemons, London and New York, 1916), p. 139.

service. It is a characteristic note of early humanism, writes W. H. Woodward, "that knowledge is desirable in proportion to the use which can be publicly made of it, and that wisdom hoarded up and not expressed partakes of selfishness." [23] Wisdom could thus serve its great purpose only if, through the art of rhetoric, it could be made at once delightful and moving. It is not merely elegance which it gives to speech, but the power of effective persuasion. The emphasis, especially of English humanism, on this practical ideal of public service is suggested by the title of the first educational treatise in the language, *The Governour*. Elyot recommends "that parte of rhethorike, principally, which concerneth persuasion: for as moche as it is moste apte for consultations." [24] Writing as a humanist, he devotes much attention to the value of eloquence. Thus learning used in the public interest as well as in the interest of the cultivated individual required the power of expression which was to be studied in the discipline of rhetoric.

The strength of the rhetorical tradition in Elizabethan culture is suggested by the principles on which the English language was criticized and judged. Early in the sixteenth century, English was considered by humanist scholars barbarous, inelegant, and lacking in copiousness. With the growth of national feeling, however, writers began to favor the use of English for patriotic reasons, and they looked to the classical writers on rhetoric for guidance. The possibilities of the English language were to be realized by studying classical languages, imitating classical authors, and more particularly, by applying the principles of rhetoric to the vernacular. "I omitt to shew," wrote Sir Humphrey Gilbert, "what ornament will therby growe to our tounge, and how able yt will appeare for strengthe and plenty when, by such exercizes [orations made in English], learning shall haue brought vnto yt the Choyce of wordes, the building of sentences, the garnishmente of figures, and other

[23] Woodward, *Studies in Education*, p. 10.
[24] *The Governour*, Everyman's Library, p. 41.

beautyes of Oratorie." [25] Some writers tried to make the English language more elegant by introducing strange words, a lesson that may have been learned from Cicero. Ralph Lever, like Sir John Cheke [26] and others, prefers that English grow from its own roots, because then its meaning is more clear. He argues in effect with Quintilian that "clearness is the first virtue of eloquence." [27] But all writers seem to agree on the necessity of expanding the language with the expansion of their intellectual horizons. Bacon defends the introduction of new words if done with restraint.[28] Jonson's opinion perhaps represents the conclusion of the wise, when he admits the value of "words borrow'd of Antiquity; . . . but," he says, drawing, like writers throughout the controversy, upon a classical rhetorician, "the eldest of the present, and the newest of the past Language is the best." [29]

The principles of rhetoric also influenced the thought of writers about other literary problems. The study of rhetoric emphasizes the significance of literary form. The early humanists fought for recognition of the importance of form, which had often been scornfully neglected by the disputants of the Middle Ages. The Ciceronians insisted on the inseparability of wisdom and eloquence, and said in effect with Crassus in *De oratore*, that "the words cannot fall into place if you remove the matter, nor can the matter have clarity if you withdraw the words." [30] For Ascham, Peacham, Sidney, and Puttenham in

[25] *Queene Elizabethes Achademy*, written after 1562, ed. Frederick J. Furnivall (London, 1869), p. 2.

[26] See the "Forespeach" to Ralph Lever, *The Arte of Reason*, 1573, and Cheke's letter to Hoby (reprinted in The Tudor Translations issue of *The Courtier*, 1900, pp. 12–13).

[27] *Institutio oratoria*, II, iii, 8 (Loeb Classical Library, I, 221); cf. *Discoveries*, in *Ben Jonson*, ed. C. H. Herford, Percy and Evelyn Simpson (10 vols., Oxford, 1925–   ), VIII, 622.

[28] *Of the Advancement of Learning*, in *Works*, ed. J. Spedding, R. L. Ellis, and D. D. Heath (15 vols., Boston, 1860–64), VI, 118–21.

[29] *Discoveries*, in *Ben Jonson*, ed. Herford and Simpson, VIII, 622; cf. *Institutio oratoria*, I, vi, 41 (Loeb Classical Library, I, 130).

[30] *De oratore*, III, v, 19 (Loeb Classical Library, II, 17).

England, the study of literary form involved the study of moral ideas, for they were inseparable. "Ye know not what hurt ye do to learning," Ascham warned, "that care not for wordes, but for matter, and so make a devorse betwixt the tong and the hart." [31] The danger of a doctrine which emphasizes form is that it is easily misunderstood. The lengths to which Ciceronians sometimes carried their attention to form were satirized by Erasmus in *Ciceronianus*. The doctrine of imitation was narrowly interpreted and the demands of decorum neglected. In many of the manuals of rhetoric, precepts and definitions were offered without much appreciation of the difficulties of good composition. To Abraham Fraunce, a follower of Ramist doctrine, rhetoric is merely the art of garnishing speech. It is purely superficial and its aims are "grace . . . delicacie . . . maiesty." After devoting most of his book to tropes and figures, he says "observe this one lesson, the more the better," and then adds, almost as an afterthought, "yet with discretion, and without affectate curiositie." [32] The importance of decorum was fully appreciated, however, by the better teachers. "Be the figure of it selfe neuer so commendable," says George Puttenham, if it is handled "indecently," "all is amisse." [33]

Though some frequently warned that knowledge of human character and judgment of subtle differences in words were prerequisite, others were inevitably more voluble on the use of rhetorical pattern and device. The partial failure of the teaching of rhetoric, and the growing awareness of failure, is exemplified by various comic characters in the early plays of Shakespeare and Jonson. The love poems of Donne, written in the nineties, represent a reaction against the rhetorical artificiality of the earlier Elizabethan lyric. In prose there was a conscious anti-Ciceronian movement, and the warning of Seneca was recalled

[31] *The Scholemaster*, in *English Works* (ed. William Aldis Wright, Cambridge, England, 1904), p. 265.
[32] Abraham Fraunce, *The Arcadian Rhetorike* (London, 1588), Sig. H 6.
[33] *The Arte of English Poesie* (ed. Gladys Doidge Willcock and Alice Walker, Cambridge, England, 1936), pp. 262–63.

that "a fellow careful about his words, and neat in his speech
. . . is busied about toys, there's no solidity in him." [34] The
stylistic ideal of the movement was to have "the most matter
with best conceyt in fewest wordes." [35] The models to imitate
were Seneca and Tacitus. Both of these authors were favorites
of Bacon. "Seneca," he observes, "giveth an excellent check to
eloquence; *Nocet illis eloquentia, quibis non rerum cupiditatem
facit, sed sui:* [eloquence does mischief when it draws men's
attention away from the matter to fix it on itself]." [36] It is the
first distemper of learning, Bacon says, "when men study words
and not matter." [37] Cicero and most of his followers never intended that they should do so, but by emphasizing form, many
rhetoricians doubtless produced that result. It is only this sophistic tendency that Bacon attacks, not the art of rhetoric itself.
It has the "duty and office," he says, "*to apply Reason to Imagination* for the better moving of the will. . . . The end of
Rhetoric is to fill the imagination to second reason, and not to
oppress it." [38] Like Aristotle, Bacon recognizes that rhetoric can
and will be used for evil purposes. But "Rhetoric can be no more
charged with the colouring of the worse part," he writes, "than
Logic with Sophistry, or Morality with Vice." [39] Bacon felt the
continuity and unity of knowledge,[40] and quotes Cicero's complaint against Socrates, that he first separated philosophy and
rhetoric.[41]

The change in feeling toward rhetoric, which apparently
took place before the publication of Bacon's *Advancement of*

[34] Robert Burton, *The Anatomy of Melancholy*, ed. Floyd Dell and Paul
Jordan-Smith (New York, 1927), p. 25; quoted by George Williamson, "Senecan Style in the Seventeenth Century," *Philological Quarterly*, XV (1936), 338.
[35] Anthony Bacon's description of the style of Tacitus; quoted by George
Williamson, place cited, p. 327.
[36] *Of the Advancement of Learning*, in *Works*, ed. Spedding, Ellis, and
Heath, VI, 310.
[37] *Ibid.*, VI, 120.   [38] *Ibid.*, VI, 297-98.   [39] *Ibid.*, VI, 299.
[40] See Karl R. Wallace, "Bacon's Conception of Rhetoric," *Speech Monographs*, III (1936), 45-46; and *Francis Bacon on Communication and Rhetoric*
(Chapel Hill, N.C., 1943), pp. 181-82.
[41] *Op. cit.*, VI, 236.

Learning, has been variously interpreted. It has been called a re-
version to classicism under the influence of Bacon and certain
continental rhetoricians; [42] a natural development of men's interests, after the first impulses of humanism, away from language
and literary form; [43] and a "maturing of English taste," accompanied by a better understanding of artistic form.[44]
The important fact that there was a change is generally recognized.

One may find in *Discoveries* a conception of rhetoric which
seems to accept at once Bacon's criticism of the preoccupation
with words, and the Ciceronian estimation of literary form.
That this at least represents, despite the commonplace character
of the book, a view which Jonson found congenial, is suggested
by the way he translates and paraphrases what he borrows, to
fit the text to the contemporary world. Appropriate proper
names are inserted; the personal "I," one may suppose, is appropriate too. Jonson translates Cicero himself in a passage
which seems to support Bacon's criticism of the Ciceronians:

Of the two (if either were to bee wisht) I would rather have a
plaine downeright wisdome, then a foolish and affected eloquence.
For what is so furious, and *Bethl'em*-like, as a vaine sound of
chosen and excellent words, without any subject of *sentence*, or
science mix'd? [45]

The only words which Jonson adds, "affected" and "*Bethl'em*-
like," elucidate Cicero's thought. The parenthetical, "if either
were to bee wisht," suggests that Cicero, and perhaps Jonson
too, is reluctant to make a choice which in practice is unnecessary. Wisdom is perhaps a *sine qua non* of good writing, but

[42] William P. Sandford, "English Rhetoric Reverts to Classicism, 1600–1650,"
Quarterly Journal of Speech, XV (1929), 503–25.

[43] Gladys Doidge Willcock, *Shakespeare as a Critic of Language* (London,
1934), p. 25.

[44] Kenneth Orne Myrick, *Sir Philip Sidney as a Literary Craftsman* (Cambridge, Mass., 1935), p. 152.

[45] *Discoveries*, in *Ben Jonson*, ed. Herford and Simpson, VIII, 574. Many
sources of Jonson's *Discoveries* are printed in the edition of Maurice Castelain
(Paris [1906]).

neither can eloquence be neglected. As Jonson says in adapting
a paragraph from Vives,

> A man should so deliver himselfe to the nature of the subject,
> whereof he speakes, that his hearer may take knowledge of his dis-
> cipline with some delight: and so apparell faire, and good matter,
> that the studious of elegancy be not defrauded; redeeme Arts
> from their rough, and braky seates, where they lay hid, and over-
> growne with thornes, to a pure, open, and flowry light: where
> they may take the eye, and be taken by the hand.[46]

Vivid additions like the last clause again suggest that Jonson
felt the justness of what he was noting down. Like Puttenham,
Jonson emphasizes the need of decorum, which involves subtle
judgments. Here again he adapts from Vives a passage on
words:

> And herein is seene their Elegance, and Propriety, when wee use
> them fitly, and draw them forth to their just strength and nature
> by way of Translation, or *Metaphore*. But in this Translation wee
> must only serve necessity (*nam temerè nihil transfertur à pru-
> denti*) or commodity, which is a kind of necessity; that is, when
> we either absolutely want a word to expresse by, and that is neces-
> sity; or when wee have not so fit a word, and that is commodity.
> As when wee avoid losse by it, and escape obscenenesse, and gaine
> in the grace and property, which helps significance.[47]

Jonson also noted and developed a passage from Seneca's
Controversies which emphasizes the difficulty of the art of
rhetoric, if it is to be used successfully outside the school:

> *Eloquence* is a great, and diverse thing: Nor did she yet ever fa-
> vour any man so much, as to become wholly his. Hee is happy,
> that can arrive to any degree of her grace. Yet there are, who
> prove themselves Masters of her, and absolute Lords . . . but in-
> deed I would no more chuse a *Rhetorician*, for reigning in a
> *Schoole*; then I would a *Pilot*, for rowing in a Pond.[48]

It is more than an academic subject to Jonson, and it has no business circumscribing a poet's liberty "within the narrow limits of

[46] *Ibid.*, VIII, 566–67.   [47] *Ibid.*, VIII, 621.   [48] *Ibid.*, VIII, 576–77.

laws." Yet Jonson does not deny the possible usefulness of these laws, for they represent, as he writes translating from Heinsius, "whatsoever Nature at any time dictated to the most happie; or long exercise to the most laborious." This "the wisdome, and Learning of *Aristotle*, hath brought into an Art: because he understood the Causes of things: and what other men did by chance or custom, he doth by reason; and not only found out the way not to erre, but the short way we should take, not to erre." [49] Jonson does not reject rhetorical discipline, but he understands its limitations. Without native judgment, study, and practice, precepts are useless.[50] But with these, they may be very helpful.

Many of Jonson's ideas on composition and other critical problems are traced directly to the rhetoricians. Cicero, Quintilian, Heinsius, and Vossius frequently contribute to his *Discoveries*. Like other Renaissance critics, he often discusses poetry and drama in terms of rhetoric. Often it is left to posterity, he says, to appreciate the art of the "true artificer, . . . his wisdom, in dividing: his subtilty, in arguing: with what strength hee doth inspire his Readers; with what sweetnesse hee strokes them: in inveighing, what sharpnesse; in Jest, what urbanity hee uses. How he doth raigne in mens affections; how invade, and breake in upon them; and makes their minds like the thing he writes." Then, turning to another division of rhetoric, he describes the "Elocution" of this ideal writer, in which the reader will "behold what word is proper: which hath ornament: which height: what is beautifully translated: where figures are fit: which gentle, which strong to shew the composition *Manly*. And how he hath avoyded faint, obscure, obscene, sordid, humble, improper, or effeminate *Phrase*; . . ." [51] Jonson's own composition transcends anything the average student could have learned from Elizabethan school exercises, and yet, like his criticism, it is of a kind that would naturally be produced by the approach to literature through the rhetorical discipline.

[49] *Ibid.*, VIII, 641. [50] *Ibid.*, VIII, 617-18. [51] *Ibid.*, VIII, 587-88.

His method of composition, he told Drummond of Hawthornden, was to write first in prose, then to translate into verse.[52] He says he acquired the habit at school. At Westminster under Camden, translating from prose to verse was a common exercise for the afternoon.

But the uses of rhetoric which will be emphasized in this study of Jonson are dependent not only upon Jonson's interest in language and his knowledge of rhetoric, but also upon the interest and knowledge of his audience. The nature of the rhetorical discipline with which many members of his audience were familiar can best be examined by studying its place in Elizabethan schools. Rhetoric was much more than a school subject. From the elaborate treatises available to the European community of scholars, many popular works in English were adapted which appealed to various levels of the population.[53] Rhetoric was at once the basis of a practical and of a liberal education. In Sir Humphrey Gilbert's plan for an academy where boys should study not "schole learninges," but "matters of accion meet for present practize, both of peace and warre," [54] provision is made for "one who shall reade and teache bothe Logick and Rethorick," [55] and exercises were to be especially in English since "the appliaunce to vse is principally in the vulgare speach." [56] But rhetoric was also the accepted approach to the study of classical literature, and literary study was intimately related to moral training. It aimed to teach how to speak, how to write, and how to read, in the broadest senses. Its purpose might be religious or cultural, as well as practical. That rhetoric should pervade the curriculum of the Elizabethan

[52] *Conversations with Drummond of Hawthornden*, in *Ben Jonson*, ed. Herford and Simpson, I, 143.

[53] Thomas Wilson seems to have preachers and lawyers in mind as readers, whereas Puttenham constantly addresses himself to a courtier. On the other hand, Edmund Coote (*The English School-Master*, 1596), William Fulwood (*The Enimie of Idlenesse*, 1568), and Angel Day (*The English Secretorie*, 1586), all of whom draw upon and apply the principles of rhetoric, address the "unlearned reader" especially, or even the "utterly ignorant."

[54] *Queene Elizabethes Achademy*, ed. Furnivall, p. 10.   [55] *Ibid.*, p. 2.
[56] *Ibid.*, p. 2.

school, although it does not always appear as a separate subject,[57] is therefore not surprising.

Rhetoric was commonly regarded as a subject for advanced study, and was an important part of the English university curriculum.[58] Elyot would have the student introduced to "the arte of Rhetorike" at about fourteen years,[59] approximately the age to enter the university. Ascham speaks of sending a student to the university "a perfite Scholer," there "to becum a fitte student, for Logicke and Rhetoricke."[60] Reading the works of Cicero and Quintilian was to follow a thorough grounding in grammar and extensive reading in prose and poetry; it was to precede professional training in law, medicine, or divinity. In practice, however, it does not seem that the whole of rhetoric was reserved for the university. The final stage of instruction at Ferrara was rhetorical, when Quintilian and Cicero were read.[61] At Liège, and probably at the Deventer school also, rhetorical principles were introduced in the fifth year.[62] In Sturm's Strasburg curriculum,[63] De oratore was begun in the fourth year, and at Eisleben, in a school founded under Melanchthon's influence, rhetorical studies were begun in the third year.[64] It was this tendency to move the study forward which made Bacon protest that even in the universities scholars "come too soon and too unripe to logic and rhetoric."[65] But he was thinking especially of requiring elaborate compositions of "minds empty and unfraught with matter." Rhetorical theory was useful in all literary pursuits, and its teaching was probably begun in simple form as soon as students were sufficiently

[57] Foster Watson, English Grammar Schools to 1660 (Cambridge, England, 1908), p. 440.

[58] Rashdall, The Universities of Europe, III, 155.

[59] The Governour, Everyman's Library, p. 41.

[60] The Scholemaster, ed. Wright, p. 237.

[61] Woodward, Studies in Education, pp. 38–45.   [62] Ibid., p. 86.

[63] Izora Scott, Controversies over the Imitation of Cicero (New York, 1910), p. 122.

[64] Woodward, Studies in Education, p. 221.

[65] Of the Advancement of Learning, in Works, ed. Spedding, Ellis, and Heath, VI, 178.

grounded in grammar to read with some attention to thought and style.

Humanist education followed similar lines all over Europe. Sturm, whose Strasburg curriculum was influential in England, had studied under Rudolph Agricola, who in turn had been a pupil of the Italian teachers Battista Guarino and Theodore Gaza.[66] The most popular textbook of rhetoric in the English schools was that of Talaeus,[67] the exponent of Ramist doctrines. The methods of teaching can best be studied in two books published by schoolmasters in the seventeenth century. John Brinsley, whose *Ludus Literarius: or, The Grammar Schoole* was published in 1612, began to teach soon after 1584, when he was graduated from Cambridge. Charles Hoole was graduated at Oxford fifty years later, and although he did not publish *A New Discovery of the Old Art of Teaching School* until 1659, he wrote it in 1637. The curricula they followed differ only in detail from those common in the sixteenth century. Both follow Ascham in recommending the exercise of double translation. They worked in the established tradition of humanist education, and the methods which they describe, if not quite typical, may be taken to represent what was generally aimed at.

In teaching the arts of language there was no attempt to separate one from the other. Reading was begun first because it was necessary to provide some store of thoughts for writing and speaking, but it was not far advanced before exercises in writing and speaking were assigned. Having learned the rudiments of Latin grammar, the students of the first form would read perhaps Aesop's *Fables* or Cicero's *Letters*. In the fourth form they might be introduced to the elements of rhetoric which would at once be applied to an analysis of their reading. Students were expected to come to a full understanding of rhetorical principles only by their application in analysis. Whatever they read in

[66] Woodward, *Studies in Education*, p. 88.
[67] John Brinsley, *Ludus Literarius; or, The Grammar Schoole*, ed. E. T. Campagnac (Liverpool and London, 1917), p. 203.

school they were required to analyze grammatically and rhetorically, observing and defining every trope and figure.[68] Thus the various kinds of tropes, figures of speech, and figures of thought, as well as the parts of a composition, were constantly illustrated. In the fifth and sixth forms, Hoole also drilled his students once a week to keep the definitions in mind.[69] Hoole describes how Ovid was taught in his school. Some four or six verses in each lesson, which the teacher considered worth remembering, were first repeated by the pupils. Then they were to "construe the whole lesson verbatim, minding the proprietie of words, and the elegancie of every phrase." After parsing every word grammatically, they were to give the "Tropes and Figures, the Derivations and Differences of some words, and relate such Histories as the proper names will hint at, which they may peruse before hand in their Dictionarie. And let them not forget [Hoole adds] to scan and prove every verse, and to note more difficult quantities of some syllables." Pupils then competed with one another in rendering the lesson into English prose, amplifying and adorning it with figures of rhetoric "all agreeing to the matter of moralitie therein couched," and retranslating it into Latin. Finally, they were permitted to "exercise their wits a little in trying who can turn the same into most varieties of English verses." [70] It was probably with some justice that the Elizabethan student referred to those authors with whose thought and style he had become thoroughly familiar as "his own." Hoole encouraged his students to observe closely the forms of expression by having them, after reading the historian Justin, describe a historical incident in English without their books, and translate it into Latin. The value of the concentrated study which translation required was certainly recognized by Renaissance teachers. Discussing the Latin-Greek translations done in his father's school, Battista Guarino

---

[68] Charles Hoole, *A New Discovery of the Old Art of Teaching School*, ed. E. T. Campagnac (Liverpool, 1913), p. 133.
[69] *Ibid.*, pp. 169 and 203.   [70] *Ibid.*, p. 162.

remarks: "Though delicate shades of meaning or beauties of expression may be overlooked by a casual reader they cannot escape a faithful translator." [71]

Composition was first taught by close imitation of Latin authors. The system of translating into English, and, later, retranslating into Latin was recommended by Ascham, Brinsley, and Hoole, as a means of teaching both Latin and English style. Analysis of classical literature on rhetorical principles made imitation easier. Details of style and thought, which on occasion might be appropriated, students were taught to enter in commonplace books as an aid to their memories.[72] Brinsley thought it too difficult for young students to make their own commonplace books, but, by consulting a collection like *Flores Poetarum*, he says, "they may use the matter of the best Authors, going farre beyond the matter which the wit of any child can conceive; sith that those bookes have in them, the choisest sayings of the very wisest of all ages." [73] Hoole suggests at least ten heads under which collections of useful material may be gathered. These are "Short Histories . . . Apologues and Fables . . . Adages . . . Hieroglyphics . . . Emblems and symbols . . . Ancient Laws and Customs . . . Witty Sentences . . . Rhetorical exornations . . . Topical places . . . Description of things natural and artificial." [74] Particular authors are suggested for each topic; for example, "Rhetorical exornations" may be collected out of Vossius, Farnaby, and Butler. Originality of thought was not demanded of students so much as an apt use of the best thought of the past on any subject. The "higher schollers" were, in addition, according to Brinsley, "to looke to elegancie, and finenesse of phrase and Composition; and so to be reading their exercises over and over,

---

[71] *De Ordine Docendi et Studendi*, tr. William H. Woodward, in *Vittorino da Feltre and Other Humanist Educators* (Cambridge, England, 1897), p. 168.
[72] Hoole, *A New Discovery*, pp. 181–82.
[73] Brinsley, *Ludus Literarius*, p. 188.
[74] Hoole, *A New Discovery*, pp. 181–82.

still correcting and amending them, never thinking an exercise well enough, untill no fault can be found, in Latine, propriety, Composition." [75] However, original thought was not always unwelcome. After using commonplace sources, Brinsley says, students "are still to adde whatsoever they can invent of their owne braine, so it be wittily and pithily." [76]

The places of invention, after Cicero and Aphthonius, were taught as part of the preparation for writing themes. [77] These and the five parts of a theme were also observed in reading the models of Aphthonius. [78] Students were expected by Brinsley to insert in the margin of their composition the "places" used for the invention of each argument, the names of the various rhetorical divisions, and of the tropes and figures used. [79] Reading and writing were thus closely interrelated, and practice in oral delivery sometimes preceded and followed the writing of themes. Hoole suggests that a teacher propound a "theme" to a group of students, in English and Latin, "and let them strive who can soonest return you the best *Exordium* in English, and then who can render it into the best Latine, and so you may proceed to the narration, and quite thorow every part of a theme." [80] After this oral extemporaneous exercise, the students were to be asked to write a theme later to be presented from memory.

Pronunciation, the fourth part of rhetoric, was emphasized by all Renaissance educators. Erasmus, Elyot, and others insist

[75] Brinsley, *Ludus Literarius*, p. 199.   [76] *Ibid.*, p. 188.   [77] *Ibid.*, p. 179.

[78] *Ibid.*, p. 184. The various types of school composition are described by Richard Rainold, *A Booke Called the Foundacion of Rhetorike*, 1563. They include, besides the theme, simple forms like the chria and fable as well as the more complex oration and declamation.

[79] *Ludus Literarius*, p. 185. Such information is frequently inserted in the margins of Elizabethan books for the reader's instruction. For example, see Alexander Silvayn, *The Orator* (tr. L. P. [Anthony Munday], 1586), or Angel Day, *The English Secretorie*, 1586. In other books, readers doubtless made such observations for themselves; cf. E. K.'s gloss to *The Shepherd's Calendar* (ed. W. L. Renwick, London, 1930, p. 20): "a prety Epanorthosis in these two verses, and withall a Paronomasia. . . ."

[80] Hoole, *A New Discovery*, p. 185.

that clear and correct pronunciation of the vernacular should be taught at an early age. In school, especially among younger students, reading aloud by the master was common. It was also taught to students as an art. Cleland in *The Institution of a Young Nobleman* describes how a boy should be taught to read "at the beginning with leisure, pausing at the full periods, and taking his breath at the broken points, lifting or basing his voice as the subject requireth and the admiration or question offereth." [81] In many schools there were readings in hall at meal time. Student declamations were often heard at weekly intervals, and both Latin and English plays produced annually, or more often. The Queen's Scholars at Westminster acted a Latin play annually, the Town Boys presenting one of their own from time to time. The Choir Boys of the Chapel Royal, the boys of St. Paul's and of the Merchant Taylors' School acted plays in English.[82] The value to the study of literature of reading aloud was also recognized. "Read the best authors by periods, viva voce," Ralph Johnson, a seventeenth-century schoolmaster advised, "thereby their stile will be secretly instilled into your minds." [83] Oral methods of teaching and the training of pronunciation and delivery had the further effect of training the pupil in careful listening. Literary education at Westminster, which Jonson attended, included an assignment to write up sermons heard on Sundays and Saints' days. The upper forms were to write in Latin verse, the fourth and third forms in Latin prose, the rest in English.[84] This kind of exercise must have had the effect of relating school training to the habits of ordinary life. There is evidence to suggest that the popularity of sermons among Elizabethans was not due so much to the desire to be edified as to the interest in the sermon as oratory.

[81] James Cleland, *The Institution of a Young Nobleman* (Oxford, 1607), p. 76; quoted by Woodward, *Studies in Education*, p. 309.

[82] Lawrence E. Tanner, *Westminster School: a History* (London, 1934), p. 6.

[83] Ralph Johnson, *The Scholar's Guide from the Accidence to the University* (London, 1665), p. 7.

[84] John Sargeaunt, *Annals of Westminster School* (London, 1898), p. 43.

Bishop Andrewes was not thinking only of the past when he said of Ezekiel's contemporaries: "They seemed to reckon of sermons no otherwise than of songs: to give them the hearing, to commende the air of them, and so let them goe. The musike of a song, and Rhetorique of a sermon, all is one." [85]

While the study of rhetoric provided an approach to literature through words, which usually meant sounds rather than printed symbols, it did not by any means exclude an interest in the moral value of literary study. In the first place, a knowledge of rhetoric was considered a means of studying and understanding more fully the morality of the Bible. In 1555, Richard Sherry wrote of tropes and figures: "They greatly profit us in reading of holy scripture, where if you be ignorant in the figurative speeches and tropes, you are like in many doubts to make but a slender solution." [86] Besides, classical literature was also studied for its moral content, and the entries in commonplace books were often of ethical rather than literary interest. Exercises in writing were a means of assimilating other men's moral ideas. "The principall end of making Theams, I take to be this," wrote Brinsley, "to furnish schollers with all stor of the choisest matter, that they may thereby learn to understand, speak or write of any ordinary Theame, Morall or Politicall, such as usually fall into discourse amongst men and in practice of life; and especially concerning vertues and vices." [87]

The significance of this kind of education can be considered from two points of view: its effect upon writers and its effect upon the reading and theater-going public. It taught writers and their reading public a respect for literary form, and an approach to its detailed study and analysis. It developed habits of close, analytical reading with an attention to details of style and their effects. Elizabethans prided themselves on an ability to

[85] Quoted by F. E. Hutchinson, "The English Pulpit from Fisher to Donne," in *Cambridge History of English Literature*, IV, 272.

[86] Richard Sherry, *A Treatise of the Figures of Grammar and Rhetorike* (London, 1555); quoted by Foster Watson, *English Grammar Schools*, p. 448.

[87] *Ludus Literarius*, p. 174.

discover hidden meanings and subtle implications of words. And they had been trained to listen as well as read. Attending a theater or a sermon, they could take a craftsman's pleasure in the freshness or fitness of a single expression. This unusual awareness of literary form, which Jonson could assume in his audience, makes possible the effects of rhetoric which will be noticed in his plays. As a result of its school training, his audience had a fresh awareness of the principles of rhetorical persuasion. Methods of amplification were broken down in their minds to specific figures like auxesis, tapinosis, antonomasia. This was a knowledge which Jonson and his audience shared. Like any realm of common knowledge, historical, literary, or religious, it provided a field of reference which might be useful in communication. Jonson, interested as he was in literary scholarship and theory, was the most likely of all Elizabethans to make use of it.

CHAPTER III

SOME USES OF RHETORIC IN LITERATURE

THE RHETORICAL CHARACTER of Elizabethan literature is notorious. In all its forms, from lyric poem to the novel, the more or less direct influence of the study of rhetoric can be felt. In later Elizabethan and Jacobean literature, if writers seem sometimes to free themselves from the formal discipline, it is probably truer to say, as Hardin Craig observes, that they have mastered it, and learned better to conceal their art. More than any other literary form, however, the drama was recognized as having a close affinity to oratory.[1] Plato and Aristotle had long since pointed that out. In the *Phaedrus*, Socrates observes that the art of rhetoric teaches only the "preliminaries of tragedy." [2] Aristotle goes further in referring the reader of the *Poetics* to the art of rhetoric for a discussion of "thought" as an element in the drama. "Under the head of Thought," he writes, "come all the effects to be produced by the language. Some of these are proof and refutation, the arousing of feelings like pity, fear, anger, and so on, and then again exaggeration and depreciation." [3] Thus, since dramatic dialogue frequently presents a conflict between characters in a particular situation, the problems of writing dramatic speech are much the same as those of rhetorical speech. Thomas Wilson pointed out that the rhetorician is concerned with questions limited to a particular time, place, and person; [4] the author of dramatic dia-

---

[1] Scaliger observes that oratory and the drama have the same end of persuasion (*Poetics*, I, i, in Frederick M. Padelford, *Select Translations from Scaliger's Poetics*, "Yale Studies in English," Vol. XXVI, New York, 1905, p. 3).
[2] *The Dialogues of Plato*, tr. B. Jowett (2 vols., New York, 1937), I, 272.
[3] *Poetics*, XIX, 2–5 (Loeb Classical Library, p. 73).
[4] *Arte of Rhetorique*, ed. G. H. Mair (Oxford, 1909), p. 1.

logue has the same immediate problem. Both dramatist and rhetorician must possess the power to move through the use of language. All dramatic action depends upon "the effects to be produced by the language" of one character addressing another. The situation may call for "proof and refutation"; then the dramatist must manipulate his dramatic creatures to speak with all the persuasive eloquence he wishes to endow them with. Or the situation may require "the arousing of feelings," and then, like the rhetorician, he must possess some understanding of human emotion in order to be able to use language effectively. The character as a literary form goes back to the sketches of Theophrastus, the rhetorician, and they seem to have been written as part of a treatise on rhetoric.[5] Aristotle's *Rhetoric* contains an important section on the analysis of character, some understanding of which was considered as essential to the rhetorician as we today consider it to the dramatist. But a character sketch, or a speech arousing pity or fear, or a piece of persuasive eloquence is not in itself dramatic. The dramatic significance depends entirely upon the situation in which the speech occurs. The good dramatist does not simply speak through one of his characters, but through the drama itself. The dramatic conflict and its outcome convey a meaning to the audience outside the ken of any one of the dramatic characters. Therefore, although dramatic speech may resemble rhetorical speech superficially, the art of the dramatist goes beyond that of the rhetorician. Rhetoric provides only the "preliminaries" of drama. Not dramatic in itself, it may be a medium of dramatic representation and expression.

Much of the early Elizabethan drama, in which rant and bombast and set speeches are so conspicuous, seems not to go beyond these "preliminaries." As in the Senecan drama and in the classical drama of sixteenth-century Italy and France, dialogue

[5] J. W. H. Atkins, *Literary Criticism in Antiquity* (2 vols., Cambridge, England, 1934), I, 155.

consists of a succession of formal recitations. Dramatic person-
ages seem to be put on the stage only to make speeches, and
these are interesting primarily as oratory. Rhetoric thus probably influenced the writing of drama directly. Classical plays
were often produced in the schools, and their speeches were re-
cited and discussed out of their contexts as examples of oratory.
Ravisius Textor, professor of rhetoric in a college at Paris, wrote
a number of Latin *Dialogi* for performance by his pupils. These
were published in 1530, and are said to have influenced the
University stage in England.[6] The medieval *conflictus* is also
pointed out as an early influence on the drama.[7] When men
began to write plays they naturally looked for models to various forms of dialogue with which they were far more familiar
than with the drama. Speeches in dialogue had long been written with the principles of oratory in mind. As the Elizabethan
drama develops, writers learn to control the rhetoric of their
language and to create an illusion of natural, animated expression. Rhetoric is made flexible so that it becomes a medium
through which truly dramatic values are produced.

The development of Jonson's use of rhetoric, however, follows different lines. Rhetorical speech in his mature comedy,
instead of being concealed, is clearly indicated to the audience.
Jonson was writing satiric drama, and the use of rhetorical
speech by a satirist was not unknown. David Worcester observes that satire "is the most rhetorical of all kinds of literature." "To succeed," he says, "it must practice the art of persuasion and become proficient with the tools of that art." [8] He
was not thinking of satiric drama, but it too must employ "the
art of persuasion," and can do so with many different effects.
Instead of addressing the reader or audience directly, the dram-

---

[6] Frederick S. Boas, *University Drama in the Tudor Age* (Oxford, 1914),
p. 19.

[7] John M. Berdan, *Early Tudor Poetry, 1485–1547* (New York, 1920), pp.
128–29.

[8] *The Art of Satire* (Cambridge, Mass., 1940), pp. 8–9.

atist addresses his characters to one another. The dramatic audience is thus made an ironic spectator of rhetorical persuasion. Rhetoric becomes a vehicle of irony. The comedy of Aristophanes is satiric drama, and like all Greek drama, is ironical.[9] The Impostor speaks in tragic bombast, or in the language of Homer, or in the special unintelligible jargon of the profession which he represents. The exaggerated character of his diction, the immediate purpose of which is deception and persuasion, is in marked contrast with the speech of the Eiron, who speaks plain Attic. The Impostor's language is rhetorical in a sense, but the audience recognizes it for the affectation which it is. Its rhetorical character is part of the dramatist's medium of expression. Similarly, when Socrates, in the *Menexenus*, delivers a funeral oration which follows closely the set form for such a speech, the reader of Plato must be critically alert to understand his true meaning. Rhetoric is only the vehicle of his irony.

In the schools of rhetoric it was a common exercise to defend the harder side of a question, and without much interest in the truth, the speakers took their arguments seriously if only they sounded plausible. In the *Phaedrus* Socrates ridicules this attitude by making a set speech to prove that a non-lover is rather to be accepted than a lover. Through his irony he raises many serious questions about the aims of rhetoric and its practitioners. The reader is not moved to believe his thesis, but is made to see through the rhetoric to another meaning which he wishes to convey. The writer who makes this kind of irony most characteristic of his style is Lucian. As a professor of rhetoric he was doubtless familiar with the practice of making orations on unlikely or unpopular subjects, and, perhaps taking the hint from Plato,[10] he introduced irony into speeches of this kind. He sometimes felt it necessary to explain his intention to the

---

[9] In the following remarks on Greek comedy I am indebted to Francis M. Cornford, *The Origin of Attic Comedy* (London, 1914), and to J. A. K. Thomson, *Irony* (Cambridge, Mass., 1927).

[10] Thomson, *Irony*, pp. 196–200.

reader,[11] which suggests how unfamiliar this kind of irony was. His satire, unlike Plato's but like that of the Old Comedy, is personal and abusive. He himself was a conscious stylist who cared more for literary effect than for truth. His method, once discovered, was simple. In writing the *Dialogues of the Gods*, he may have said to himself, as Messrs. Fowler suppose, "let us put the thing into plain natural prose, and see what it looks like with its glamour of poetry and reverence stripped off." [12] Or, on the other hand, in writing about the fly, where it was least expected, he would add "the glamour of poetry and reverence."

The possible variations are limitless and the great possibilities of such irony are perhaps best suggested by the orations, *Phalaris I* and *Phalaris II*. In the first a tyrant offers, through his ambassadors, a gift to the priests of Apollo at Delphi. In his oration, Phalaris defends his tyranny and cruelty as necessary and just, and offers the gift as a monument of his justice. It is a golden bull made by Perilaus in a desire to please his ruler. To be used as an incinerator for Phalaris's enemies, it was equipped so that their groans, blowing through the bull's nostrils, would make music for Phalaris's ears. Phalaris boasts that he burned Perilaus himself in it, as a just punishment for his cruel design, and was now offering it as a gift to Apollo as a sign of his often misunderstood justice. The propriety and dignity of the speech are in ironic contrast with the character of the act which it represents. The second oration, a dramatic outcome of the first, is a speech by one of the priests arguing that the gift should be accepted. All of his arguments are to be understood ironically; the most prominent is: "if you make yourselves examiners and inquisitors upon gifts, I doubt we shall be in want of people to examine hereafter." [13]

In the Middle Ages rhetoric continued to provide a literary

[11] At the beginning of *A True Story* he says, "I tell all kinds of lies in a plausible and specious way" (Loeb Classical Library, I, 249).

[12] "Introduction" to *The Works of Lucian of Samosata*, tr. H. W. and F. G. Fowler (4 vols., Oxford, 1905), p. xxv.

[13] *Phalaris II* (Loeb Classical Library, I, 31).

field of reference for school celebrations and material for writers of satire. One such celebration lasted in England until Queen
Elizabeth's reign; Puttenham alludes to it:

> on Saint *Nicholas* night commonly the Scholars of the Countrey
> make them a Bishop, who like a foolish boy, goeth about blessing
> and preaching with so childish termes, as maketh the people laugh
> at his foolish counterfaite speeches.[14]

St. Nicholas was the patron saint of scholars and children, and
such a celebration with processions, revels, and masquerades
was widespread in the Middle Ages. One of the most popular
details of the celebration was the election by the children in a
school or parish of a Boy Bishop who, for the occasion, was
accorded some of the honors of a real dignitary. He led processions through the town, blessing the inhabitants, and on Chil-
dermas day preached a sermon in the church. The source of
humor, as in Lucian, lay in the incongruity of his speech. It was
by a deliberate failure to observe rhetorical decorum that the
"bishop" made "the people laugh at his foolish counterfaite
speeches." This sort of humor was a natural product of the
study of rhetoric in all times and places. In this popular form
the subtlety of irony was probably rare, but that it was not
unknown in medieval literature is shown by Chaucer's *Nun's
Priest's Tale*.[15]

In the sixteenth century the English rhetoric books often
show an acute awareness of an affected, inapt, and hopelessly
ineffective use of rhetorical knowledge. This is especially true
later in the century when the attitude toward the subject became more critical. In the second edition of his *Garden of Eloquence*, published in 1593, Peacham added, after his description
of each figure, certain "cautions" about their misuse. These

---

[14] *Arte of English Poesie*, ed. Gladys Doidge Willcock and Alice Walker
(Cambridge, England, 1936), p. 273. An account of this celebration is given by
E. K. Chambers, *The Mediaeval Stage* (2 vols., Oxford, 1903), I, 336–71.

[15] J. M. Manly ("Chaucer and the Rhetoricians," *Proceedings of the British
Academy*, 1926), describes Chaucer's development in relation to rhetorical
doctrines. Chaucer "came more and more to make only a dramatic use of these
rhetorical elements, that is, to put them into the mouths of his *dramatis personae* and to use only such as might fittingly be uttered by them" (p. 18).

often contain "foolish" or "ridiculous" examples of the use of a figure, which are admittedly humorous. In discussing Ecphonesis, he says "it were ridiculous to begin a publicke speech with this figure, crying, O, or Alasse: it might sooner move laughter then lamentation." Nor, he adds, ought it be "put in conclusion of an oration or publicke speech, for in so doing it might be the cause of merry effect." [16] The new critical attitude toward the figures is suggested also by his warning about the use of synecdoche "among cavilling and captious persons, which of wilful perversenesse may easily pervert the true meaning, either by malice or mockerie." The cautions would have been unnecessary were the abuses which Peacham describes unreal. His examples, however, would only include the most conspicuous and most common faults in rhetorical usage. A literary artist with greater sensitiveness to language may have observed more subtle and more telling faults, and in writing may have invented a context for them, as Lucian and Chaucer had done, which could make them serve a serious artistic purpose.

Although there was a growing consciousness of stylistic abuses toward the end of the century, earlier rhetoricians were not unaware of them. Thomas Wilson in *The Arte of Rhetorique* issues a warning against affected writing: "I know them," he says, "that thinke *Rhetorique* to stande wholie vpon darke wordes, and hee that can catche an ynke horne terme by the taile, him they coumpt to be a fine Englisheman, and a good *Rhetorician*." [17] A product of humanist training at Cambridge, Wilson had studied other subjects as well as rhetoric, and had retained a sense of proportion. Puttenham's emphasis on decorum has already been mentioned, and like Peacham he shows an appreciation for the humorous possibilities of a failure to observe it. He devotes many pages to a series of anecdotes on the subject, in which his purpose is not so much instruction as delight, not "to tell you of all the partes of decencie and indecency," he says, but "rather to solace your eares with pretie conceits after a sort of long scholasticall preceptes which may

---

[16] *Garden of Eloquence*, 1593, p. 63.   [17] Ed. G. H. Mair, p. 162.

happen haue doubled them." [18] His tales are thus told for their intrinsic interest, though they are all based upon the failure to observe a rhetorical principle.[19] Such material was already being used in the Renaissance literature of satire.

The traditional practice in the schools of making orations on unpromising subjects was not unknown in the Renaissance. John Jewel, Prelector in Humanities and Rhetoric at Oxford, delivered an *Oratio contra Rhetoricam* which is probably to be taken as a "*tour de force* of mingled irony, burlesque, and rhetorical display, with perhaps a modicum of serious intent." [20] Under the influence of Lucian, according to J. A. K. Thomson,[21] the use of such a form for purposes of satire had reappeared in Erasmus's *Praise of Folly*. In it rhetoric is used as a vehicle of irony, a medium through which the author insinuates his meaning to a sophisticated audience. The reader is compelled to attend constantly to the style, but he must also see beyond it. It must be seen in the perspective of the subject matter and the speaker. Rabelais also is a writer who, as Baldwin observes, "will not let us ever forget his style"; [22] full of oratory, of legal and medical jargons, of Latin terminology, dialect, and slang, his style is only a means to an end. Language is the material of his art in more than one sense. The special kind of language in which he writes is the medium through which satire takes effect.

Like Puttenham, Jonson stresses the importance of decorum, and it is a principle which applies to the drama as well as ora-

[18] *Arte of English Poesie*, ed. Willcock and Walker, p. 276.

[19] Horace points out the comic effect of a failure to observe decorum. See in Jonson's translation, *Horace his Art of Poetrie* (in *Ben Jonson*, ed. Herford and Simpson, VIII, 313):

> "If now the phrase of him that speakes, shall flow
> In sound, quite from his fortune; both the rout,
> And Roman Gentrie, jearing, will laugh out."

[20] Hoyt H. Hudson, "Jewel's Oration against Rhetoric: a Translation," *Quarterly Journal of Speech*, XIV (1928), 375.

[21] "Erasmus in England," in *England und die Antike*, ed. Fritz Saxl (Leipzig and Berlin, 1932), pp. 64–82.

[22] Charles Sears Baldwin, *Renaissance Literary Theory and Practice* (New York, 1939), p. 202.

tory. This "figure of figures," as Hoskyns calls it,[23] requires that "all circumstances of the person, place, time, cause and purpose" [24] be taken into account. But the dramatist must go beyond this to consider the effect of his stage argument on the audience. In the observance of decorum, Jonson found an important means of revealing and representing character. Decorum applies equally to speech and to action, both of which the dramatist uses. It is speech which especially interests Jonson: "No glasse renders a mans forme, or likenesse, so true as his speech," he wrote.[25] The style of men's speech is as varied as the quality of their minds, and in an age when speech was cultivated by the study of rhetoric, the quality of a man's art in speaking was a mark of his character, to one who could see it. "Wheresoever, manners, and fashions are corrupted, Language is. It imitates the publicke riot. The excesse of Feasts, and apparell, are the notes of a sick State; and the wantonnesse of language, of a sick mind." [26] The comic dramatist especially, who "imitates the publicke riot" on the stage, draws upon men's speech, for of all men, as Jonson says, the fool reveals himself most quickly by his language: "The treasure of a foole is alwayes in his tongue." [27] The vices of comic characters can be most easily represented to an audience by the vices of their speech: "There is almost no man, but hee sees clearlier, and sharper, the vices in a speaker, then the vertues. And there are many, that with more ease, will find fault with what is spoken foolishly, then that can give allowance to that wherein you are wise silently." [28] The fact that comedy treats of common life, and represents the character and affections of ordinary men, led Jonson to the conviction that of all poets "the *Comicke* comes neerest" the orator:

[23] John Hoskyns, "Directions for Speech and Style" in Louise Brown Osborn, *Life, Letters, and Writings of John Hoskyns,* in "Yale Studies in English," Vol. LXXXVII (New Haven, 1937), p. 129.

[24] George Puttenham, *Arte of English Poesie,* ed. Willcock and Walker, p. 155.

[25] *Discoveries,* in *Ben Jonson,* ed. Herford and Simpson, VIII, 625.

[26] *Ibid.,* VIII, 593.   [27] *Ibid.,* VIII, 575.   [28] *Ibid.,* VIII, 575.

Because [he says], in moving the minds of men, and stirring of affections (in which Oratory shewes, and especially approves her eminence) hee chiefly excells. What figure of a Body was *Lysippus* ever able to forme with his Graver, or *Apelles* to paint with his Pencill, as the Comedy to life expresseth so many, and various affections of the minde? There shall the Spectator see some, insulting with Joy; others, fretting with Melancholy; raging with Anger; mad with Love; boiling with Avarice; undone with Riot; tortur'd with expectation; consum'd with feare: no perturbation in common life, but the Orator findes an example of it in the Scene.[29]

Like Quintilian, Jonson especially commends the language used by the comic dramatists, though he mentions Plautus rather than writers of the Old Comedy. Both Jonson and Quintilian (in the passage which Jonson seems to have in mind) [30] are thinking of the use of comic literature by the orator rather than the use of oratory by comic poets.

In the drama, which imitates life, the strict observance of decorum may involve what, on the level of real life and of oratory, is a failure to observe decorum. The speech of fools must be foolish to be correct. And here Jonson observes a "special Decorum," as he claimed to do in presenting *Bartholomew Fair* not where it was supposed to take place, but in the theater, "the place being as durty as *Smithfield*, and as stinking euery whit." [31] A rhetorical vice is often turned into a dramatic virtue. "You are not," Jonson warns in *Discoveries*, "to cast a Ring for the perfumed termes of the time," [32] but the speech of several characters in his earlier plays is marked by these terms. Perspicuity is often endangered, he notes, "by affectation of some wit ill angled for, or ostentation of some hidden termes of Art. Few words they darken speech, and so doe too many." [33] In his dramatic language Jonson often fails deliberately to ob-

[29] *Ibid.*, VIII, 640–41.

[30] *Institutio oratoria*, X, i, 65 (Loeb Classical Library, IV, 36–38).

[31] *Bartholomew Fair*, "The Induction" (*Ben Jonson*, ed. C. H. Herford, Percy and Evelyn Simpson, 10 vols., Oxford, 1925– , VI, 17).

[32] *Discoveries*, in *Ben Jonson*, ed. Herford and Simpson, VIII, 632.

[33] *Ibid.*, VIII, 631.

serve this warning. The failure is a rhetorical vice, not only parodied as literary satire, but made to produce more strictly dramatic values. Jonson would surely have sympathized with Sperone Speroni when he said:

I grieve at the wretched condition of these modern times, in which study is spent not in being but in seeming wise. . . . We think we know something well enough when, without comprehending its nature, we are able to give it the name given by Cicero, Pliny, Lucretius, Vergil, or Plato, Aristotle, Demosthenes, Aeschines.[34]

We shall find such "names" characteristic of Jonson's dramatic language. For, as already observed, he was aware like Erasmus of the limitations and abuses of the art of speaking, as it was taught in the rhetorical tradition. "*An Innocent* man needs no *Eloquence*," he wrote.[35] Jonson could follow no tradition blindly. Of the two fools in *Epicoene*, Dauphine says, "They haue nothing, not the vse of their senses, but by tradition." [36]

Jonson's satire, like that of Lucian and Erasmus, goes beyond ridicule of mere literary affectation, though this is characteristic of some early plays of Jonson as well as Shakespeare and other contemporaries. The satiric purge in *Poetaster* is an example, and it was borrowed from Lucian.[37] What seems more characteristic of Jonson's greatest achievement, however, is the irony which, like the irony of Lucian and Erasmus, is partly effected by manipulation of the art of rhetoric.

The irony of Jonson's outlook appears not only in his plays. In the *Conversations with Drummond of Hawthornden*, for example, Jonson said he had written a satire on the times lamenting that "there was no abuses to writte a Satyre of." [38] "*I have* considered, our whole life is like a *Play*," he wrote in *Dis-*

---

[34] *Dialogo delle lingue*, ed. 1596, p. 126; quoted by C. S. Baldwin, *Renaissance Literary Theory and Practice*, p. 26.

[35] *Discoveries*, in *Ben Jonson*, ed. Herford and Simpson, VIII, 604.

[36] *Epicoene*, III, iii, 98–99 (V, 207).

[37] Jonson's debt to Lucian is studied by Joseph Quincy Adams, "The Sources of Ben Jonson's *Volpone*," *Modern Philology*, II (1904–5), 289–99. His debt to Erasmus is studied in John D. Rea's edition of *Volpone* ("Yale Studies in English," Vol. LIX, New Haven, Conn., 1919).

[38] *Conversations*, ed. Herford and Simpson, I, 135.

coveries, "wherein every man forgetfull of himselfe, is in tra-
vaile with expression of another." [39] In other words, the world is
full of impostors. But, Jonson adds, "though the most be Players,
some must be *Spectators*." These latter, the great, good men,
observe the world as ironists. Speaking again of the world as he
observed it, Jonson says: ". . . wee take pleasure in the lye, and
are glad, wee can cousen our selves. Nor is it onely in our wals,
and seelings; but all that wee call happinesse, is meere painting,
and guilt: and all for money: what a thinne Membrane of
honour that is?" [40] The world which Jonson describes in these
passages is the world of his comedy, and it has many interesting
parallels to the Old Comedy, which is one of the earliest forms
of literature in which rhetoric is used with the effect of irony.
The remark of Cordatus that *Every Man Out of His Humor*
is "somewhat like *Vetus Comoedia*" is shown by O. J. Campbell to mean that Jonson actually was then imitating the old
Greek comedy.[41] Jonson's later plays, including *Volpone* and
The Alchemist, also show some resemblances to the Old
Comedy. Cornford divides the characters of the Old Comedy
into three types, according to an Aristotelian tradition: the
Buffoon, the Ironical Type, and the Impostor.[42] Campbell has
shown how in his Comical Satires Jonson's characters may be
so classified.[43] His later characters also have much in common
with the Eiron and Alazon of Old Comedy. "The word *eiron*

[39] Ed. Herford and Simpson, VIII, 597. Cf. Erasmus: "And what is all this
Life but a kind of Comedy, wherein men walk up and down in one another's
Disguises, and Act their respective Parts, till the property-man brings 'em
back to the Tyring House" (*The Praise of Folly*, ed. Mrs. P. S. Allen, Oxford,
1913, p. 53).

[40] *Discoveries*, in *Ben Jonson*, ed. Herford and Simpson, VIII, 607–608.

[41] O. J. Campbell says that Renaissance critics applied the term *vetus comoedia* "to the Greek comedy which culminated in the work of Aristophanes,
and to nothing else" (*Comicall Satyre and Shakespeare's Troilus and Cressida*,
San Marino, Calif., 1938, p. 4).

[42] This is the classification of the *Tractatus Coislinianus* (Lane Cooper, *An
Aristotelian Theory of Comedy, with an Adaptation of the Poetics and a
Translation of the "Tractatus Coislinianus,"* New York, 1922, p. 226). The
first two types have much in common and often combine in order to expose
the Impostor (Cornford, *Origin of Attic Comedy*, p. 138).

[43] Campbell, *Comicall Satyre*, p. 57.

itself in the fifth century [Cornford writes] appears to mean 'cunning' or (more exactly) 'sly.' Especially it meant the man who masks his batteries of deceit behind a show of ordinary good nature." [44] In this sense Volpone and Subtle are ironical types, and, like the type in ancient comedy, they practice deception partly for their own private satisfaction in exposing human folly. The other important class of characters in the Old Comedy is that of Impostors who are "impudent and absurd pretenders." Among them we have a "whole gallery of quacks and humbugs standing for various professional classes in society" [45]—the Boastful Soldier, the Learned Doctor, the Cook, the Parasite, all of whom and more appear in Jonsonian comedy. Jonson surpasses the Old Comedy in irony when, in his mature plays, even his ironists are impostors or dupes. The impostors are divided only according to their wit. The action as well as the characters of a Jonsonian comedy, especially in its earlier forms, as Campbell has shown, has some resemblance to the Old Comedy. The Impostors exhibit themselves in a series, and their absurdities are drawn out by the Eiron, who victimizes and exposes them. The audience which knows that the Impostor is doomed to exposure assumes the role of ironist. Jonson's audience often takes the same pleasure in an episode as the knavish characters themselves. A refinement of Jonson's dramatic irony is that his fools and impostors are usually responsible for their own exposure, tying the noose around their own necks.

The critical attitude which Jonson constantly demands from his audience is in fact the attitude of the ironist. Dramatic irony is the spectator's sense of clash "between appearance and reality in events or language." [46] In Jonson the language of rhetoric is used frequently with this dramatic effect. When words are analyzed in their contexts, dramatic irony reveals itself in deeper and deeper layers. The technique of irony which seems most characteristic of Jonson's style is the use of rhetorical speech.

[44] Cornford, *Origin of Attic Comedy*, p. 137.   [45] *Ibid.*, p. 140.
[46] G. G. Sedgewick, *Of Irony, Especially in Drama* (Toronto, 1935), p. 26.

CHAPTER IV

THE NATURE OF JARGON
AND ITS USE IN JONSON'S
EARLIER PLAYS

WHEN A theater audience perceives more of the true situation and is conscious of perceiving more than the characters of a play, the effective result is dramatic irony. The irony of Jonson's plays is often dependent upon the audience's perception of the quality of a dramatic speech. His audience is required to recognize the rhetorical character of language when some of the stage persons fail to do so. Such language is frequently commented upon in the dialogue for the benefit of the audience, but the education in rhetoric which had trained the Elizabethans to direct their attention to language, and had made them aware of the methods of persuasion, had prepared them also to make the needed response to Jonson's plays. The study of rhetorical amplification had taught them a special awareness of the "words," "terms," or "names" by which persuasive speech often works. The frequency with which the word "term" appears in Elizabethan writing in this rhetorical sense suggests the Elizabethan awareness of rhetorical values in words. When the Clown in *Twelfth Night* says to the possessed Malvolio, "Fie, thou dishonest Satan! I call thee by the most modest terms," [1] he shows by the apology for his choice of words (which is itself a rhetorical device) that he expected "dishonest Satan" to be recognized as "terms" chosen for their rhetorical value. In *The Merry Wives* when Ford is touched by jealousy he reflects:

---

[1] IV, ii, 35–36. All references to Shakespeare's plays are to *The Complete Works*, ed. George Lyman Kittredge (Boston, 1936).

See the hell of having a false woman! My bed shall be abus'd, my coffers ransack'd, my reputation gnawn at; and I shall not only receive this villanous wrong, but stand under the adoption of abominable terms, and by him that does me this wrong. Terms! names! Amaimon sounds well; Lucifer, well; Barbason, well; yet they are devils' additions, the names of fiends. But cuckold! wittol! Cuckold! the devil himself hath not such a name.[2]

It is not only the simple fact that he considers. He seems even more concerned with the sound and the rhetorical effect of the terms which may describe him. The word "term" appears in Shakespeare most commonly in this sense; such "terms" are highly characteristic of the language of Jonson's plays. Recognized as such by his audience, they are productive of dramatic irony.

It is a commonplace that Jonson's dramatic imagination was more stirred by the knavery and folly in men than by the vices and virtues. His work as a whole may be looked upon as a great satire upon human ignorance.[3] Ignorance and folly must have revealed themselves to him frequently in the quality of men's speech; he observes in *Discoveries* that "*Language* most shewes a man." [4] The language which exhibits ignorance or folly should have provided him with a useful dramatic speech. "The monster ignorance," he wrote in a note on one of his masques, "still couets, to enwrap it selfe in darke, and obscure tearmes, and betray that way." [5] Here in the allegorical language of the masque, Jonson describes a quality of speech which is a sign of the ignorant. In his plays he translates this "monster ignorance"

---

[2] II, ii, 305–14.

[3] In the chain of vices described in *The Masque of Queens*, Note "n," Ignorance is placed first, because "the opposition to all *vertue* begins out of *Ignorance*" (*Ben Jonson*, ed. C. H. Herford, Percy and Evelyn Simpson, 10 vols., Oxford, 1925– , VII, 287). All references to Jonson's plays and masques are to this edition; volume and page are given in parentheses immediately following the citation.

[4] *Discoveries*, in *Ben Jonson*, ed. Herford and Simpson, VIII, 625. Jonson adapted the idea from Apuleius and Vives. In the *Conversations with Drummond*, he censures Sidney because he "did not keep a Decorum jn making every one speak as well as himself" (Herford and Simpson, I, 132).

[5] *Love Freed from Ignorance and Folly*, Note "a" (VII, 362).

into varieties of human beings who, as learned doctors (of alchemy, divinity, and the law, for instance), use their "tearmes" to prey upon a still lower order of ignorance, and "betray that way." Such language depends for its success upon a rhetorical skill which is not at all incompatible with real ignorance. Jonson was one of many students of rhetoric who observed that rhetorical speech is often thus abused, but no other Elizabethan dramatist makes such frequent and powerful use of the fact.

Technical language in Jonson is usually what we should more accurately call technical jargon. Such language which is not used as a jargon is rare in his plays, and is certainly not a marked characteristic of his style. The frequent appearance of special terms in Jonson's verse, and the accuracy of their use, are often mentioned as evidence of his wide and deep knowledge, and of his personal delight in displaying it. When words are examined in their dramatic contexts, however, both of these conclusions seem doubtful. Most technical terms in Jonson are used by knaves, who exploit them as convincing rhetoric; by fools, who innocently believe they indicate learning; or by critics, who use them in satiric description. In all cases there is an implication that the terms are easily picked up, and are more often a sign of ignorance than of learning. It is unlikely that Jonson was so uncritical of himself that he fell into an affectation which he constantly ridicules. But even though these terms are used by Jonson critically as an affectation, they do indicate a wide range of reading, and an interest in the specialized languages of various groups.

A metaphor which Jonson used to describe all kinds of specialized jargon has become a part of the language. The word "canting" originally designated the whining intonation of beggars, but was extended in the sixteenth century to include the unintelligible secret jargon of gipsies, beggars, and thieves. Jonson contributed to the further growth of the word. After his time it could mean "the use of the special phraseology of a particular class or subject." [6] The word is most clearly defined by Jonson in *The Staple of News*. Pennyboy Junior's father, disguised as a beggar, is called Pennyboy Canter, and is described for the ear of the audience as "*a kin to the* Poet." [7] His criticism of the "jeerers" makes them turn their railing against him, and they ridicule his language.

FIT[TON]. This Rogue, this *Canter!*
P[ENIBOY] IV[NIOR].   O, good words.
FIT.   A fellow
     That speakes no language—
ALM[ANACH].   But what gingling *Gipsies*,
     And *Pedlers* trade in—
FIT.   And no honest *Christian*
     Can vnderstand—
P[ENIBOY] CA[NTER].   Why? by that argument,
     You all are *Canters*, you, and you, and you,
     All the whole world are *Canters*, I will proue it
     In your *professions*.[8]

When Piedmantle, the herald, appears in a later scene, and uses the technical terms of his profession, Pennyboy Canter asks, "Is not this *canting?* doe you vnderstand him?" [9] When he is called on to prove how the doctor, soldier, poet, and courtier are canters too, he does so simply by accumulating the terms of their respective professions. Thus he describes examples of the kind of language which Jonson had frequently used as dramatic speech. Throughout most of his career Jonson had represented men whose pretense to knowledge of various kinds was carried out, often with ingenuity and success, through an affectation of terms. The last of the "jeerers" whom Pennyboy Canter ridicules is the courtier, whose "*mynt-phrase*," he says, is "the worst of *canting*." Jargon is not limited by Jonson to the speech

[6] *The New English Dictionary* credits Jonson with the first use of "canting" and "to cant" in this sense. "Cant" in a corresponding sense is first used, according to the *NED*, by T. Burnet (1684).
[7] *The Staple of News*, "The fourth Intermeane after the fourth *Act*," 4–5 (VI, 362).
[8] *Ibid.*, IV, i, 51–57 (VI, 347).   [9] *Ibid.*, IV, iv, 27 (VI, 357).

of the learned professions, nor to any particular class. He must have felt the truth of Pennyboy Canter's contention that "All the whole world are *Canters.*" His quarrel with all kinds of canting was that "it affects the *sense,* it has not." [10] Such language actually is rhetoric in a common modern sense of the word, and when Jonson says the poet "*is no subiect for pride and ignorance to exercise their rayling rhetorique vpon,*" [11] he is using "rhetorique" in a similar sense. Out of such an "exercise" used by "pride and ignorance" to conceal the truth Jonson created a dramatic speech.

In the address "To the Reader" of *The Alchemist,* Jonson speaks of the "Professors" of poetry who now "*are deriders of all diligence*" in art, "*and, by simple mocking at the termes, when they vnderstand not the things, thinke to get of wittily with their Ignorance. Nay, they are esteem'd the more learned, and sufficient for this, by the Many, through their excellent vice of iudgement.*" [12] The "Professors" and the "Many" form the two largest classes among Jonson's characters. The "darke, and obscure termes" used by "the monster ignorance" to "betray that way" have already been defined. In the plays, the "Professors" often do indeed "*get of wittily with their Ignorance,*" and Jonson shows little sympathy for their dupes whose "*excellent vice of iudgement*" makes them the prey of anyone capable of speaking a few "*termes.*" The dupes constantly confuse words and things; they fail to inquire into the meaning of the words they hear, and are impressed by mere sounds. Worst of all they themselves affect the use of the terms and their speech has no basis in knowledge. If Jonson in *Discoveries* had not explicitly commended Bacon's warning about the confusion between words and things, the evidence of the plays would have been sufficient to indicate his conscious acceptance of the same view. The identification of the word with the thing it represents, and of learned terms with learning, al-

[10] *Ibid.,* IV, iv, 75 (VI, 359).   [11] *Volpone,* "The Epistle," 30–31 (V, 17).
[12] *The Alchemist,* "To the Reader," 11–15 (V, 291).

though a common human failing, was encouraged further, as Bacon observed, by the kind of training which a rhetorical education entailed. Students who were taught to treasure words and phrases in commonplace books may easily have learned to place a false value upon them. The common distinction among orators between word and thing [13] was often merely a verbal distinction.

In the Preface to *Joseph Andrews*, Fielding says that "affection proceeds from one of these two causes, vanity or hypocrisy," and he observes that Jonson "hath chiefly used the hypocritical affectation." [14] In his early plays, however, Jonson uses a language full of vain affectations of speech which rhetorical education fostered among Elizabethan gentlemen. Although a gentleman's vocabulary was not limited in scope to one set of technical terms, he too, like the professional man, had a "canting" language in which there was a wide discrepancy between the sound and the sense. In Jonson the language of gallants and their gulls is characterized primarily by literary affectation. In their vainly affected speech, they commonly abused words by straining their meaning. When Sogliardo thus abuses the word "humour," Cordatus comments ironically: "O, beare with him, and he should lacke matter, and words too, 'twere pittifull." [15] Such language handled skillfully may be effective, however, in impressing the ignorant. Fastidious admires the "plentifull discourse" of Saviolina, which Carlo Buffone describes as "nothing but sound, sound, a meere *eccho;* . . . good enough to catch flies withall." [16] This language has in effect obvious affinities to the professional jargons. The most vainly affected speech has a purpose like sophisti-

---

[13] The distinction is frequently made by Jonson's characters, sometimes legitimately, sometimes not. Compare Cordus's use of it (*Sejanus*, III, 407–408; Herford and Simpson, IV, 406) with Afer's (*Sejanus*, III, 173–75; Herford and Simpson, IV, 398).

[14] *Joseph Andrews*, ed. George Saintsbury (2 vols., London, 1893), I, xlii–xliii.

[15] *Every Man Out of His Humor*, II, i, 58–59 (III, 461).

[16] *Ibid.*, II, iii, 208–10 (III, 476).

cated rhetoric of impressing the hearer. When Amorphus instructs Asotus in speaking, he advises him to remember any "new *phrase*" or "acute jest" he may hear, and use it as his own. Asotus fears he cannot repeat it perfectly, but Amorphus assures him: "No matter, let it come lame. In ordinary talke you shall play it away, as you doe your light crownes at *primero:* It will passe." [17] This language is the gallant's rhetoric. If it is not learned by imitating what has been observed, it may be had from a book; such learning, Horace in *Poetaster* says, in contrasting it with Virgil's, "most consists in *ecchoing* wordes, and termes." [18] The words which the gallants especially favored were those which seemed to indicate the education of a gentleman. Often like Lady Maria and "your ignorant *Poetasters*," "when they haue got acquainted with a strange word, [they] neuer rest till they haue wroong it in, though it loosen the whole fabricke of their sense." [19] In addition to such words, "Your *pedant* should prouide you some parcells of *french*," as Amorphus advises Asotus,"or some pretty commoditie of *italian* to commence with, if you would be exoticke, and exquisite." [20] Finally, gallants were expected to have the distinctive vocabularies of various gentlemanly pursuits. The importance which they attached to the terms as distinguished from real knowledge is emphasized in a revision Jonson made in *Every Man in His Humor*. In the Quarto, Stephano says: ". . . and a man haue not skill in hawking and hunting now a daies, ile not giue a rush for him; hee is for no gentlemans company. . . ." [21] This becomes in the Folio: ". . . an' a man haue not skill in the hawking, and hunting-languages now a dayes, I'll not giue a rush for him. They are more studied then the *Greeke,* or the *Latine.* He is for no gallants companie without 'hem." [22] The gallant's ideal was not unlike Cicero's Orator. He was to be "A pretty Scholler," as Pennyboy Junior describes Tom Barber in recommend-

[17] *Cynthia's Revels*, III, i, 47–49 (IV, 83).   [18] *Poetaster*, V, i, 130 (IV, 293).
[19] *Cynthia's Revels*, II, iv, 15–18 (IV, 77).   [20] *Ibid.*, III, v, 91–94 (IV, 97).
[21] *Every Man in His Humor*, Quarto of 1601, I, i, 38–40 (III, 198).
[22] *Ibid.*, Folio of 1616, I, i, 41–44 (III, 305).

ing him, "alike skil'd in euery *liberall Science*, As hauing certaine snaps of all." [23] In the same play, *The Staple of News*, Jonson makes clear his own attitude toward the peculiar affectations of gentlemen. When Dr. Almanach commends Madrigal for writing like a gentleman, not a scholar, Pennyboy Canter complains:

> Pox o' your distinction!
> As if a *Scholler* were no *Gentleman*.
> With these, to write like a *Gentleman*, will in time
> Become, all one, as to write like an *Asse*.[24]

This language of the gallants is most conspicuous in Jonson's early plays, and seems to lead the way to the hypocritical affectations characteristic of the language of his dramatic maturity.

Jargon in Ben Jonson's plays is here understood to consist, with rare exceptions, of two kinds of affected speech. The more important in the mature comedies is the language of "Professors" of all kinds. It is used by knaves deliberately to persuade, and by fools vainly. A less important class of characters, the critics, may use it ironically. There is secondly the language of gentlemen, which is more prominent in Jonson's early comedies, and in the works of his contemporaries. Like the professional jargons, it may be affected by knaves, fools, or critics with various motives. The use of these two kinds of affected language in particular dramatic contexts is the subject of this and the following chapter. Jonson's purpose is not merely satiric ridicule of the language itself; such language, the true character of which is recognized by the audience, but not by all the persons of the drama, is part of a technique of dramatic irony. Jonson's use of this technique in his mature plays is anticipated in simple form in his earliest comedies.

In what appear to be the earlier parts of *A Tale of a Tub* [25]

[23] *The Staple of News*, I, v, 125–32 (VI, 297–98).
[24] *Ibid.*, IV, ii, 149–52 (VI, 352).
[25] It is the consensus of opinion, based on internal evidence, that this play is Elizabethan. Herford and Simpson (I, 288) suggest 1596–97 as a probable

Jonson has followed among other dramatic conventions of the time the use of affected speech for satirical purposes. When he makes his clownish characters blunder in the use of words, deliberately misunderstand, or pun, he is following a tradition well established in the drama. It is by appealing to this already developed interest of the Elizabethan audience that Jonson begins to use a dramatic speech to which the audience is to make a critical response. The affectations of Miles Metaphor, which have close parallels in early Elizabethan drama, are dramatic only in the sense that they are a characteristic iodiosyncrasy of speech.

MET[APHOR].　Come gentle Mistris, will you please to walke?
AWD[REY].　I love not to be led: I'd goe alone.
MET.　Let not the mouse of my good meaning, Lady,
　　　　Be snap'd up in the trap of your suspition,
　　　　To loose the taile there, either of her truth,
　　　　Or swallow'd by the Cat of misconstruction.
AWD.　You are too finicall for me; speake plaine Sir.[26]

In *Discoveries* Jonson warns against too long drawing out an allegory, "lest we make our selves obscure, or fall into affectation, which is childish." His audience here recognized the allegory as comic. The quality of the language, by creating in the audience a superior and detached attitude, produces a simple kind of irony. The language of Miles Metaphor, however, has no bearing on the development of the plot.

Some of the dramatic situations of *A Tale of a Tub*, involving disguises, plots of gulling and counterplots, could have been represented with the kind of rhetorical language Jonson later employs, but apart from the simple, traditional irony of Miles Metaphor, Jonson has not yet discovered the dramatic values of rhetorical speech. If certain passages of an artificial rhetorical character are read in the light of Jonson's later work, there is a possibility of misreading. Squire Tub makes love to Audrey in

date. In its present form the play is a revision of the original text for performance in 1633.

[26] *A Tale of a Tub*, IV, iv, 23–29 (III, 70).

such a conventionally poetic strain that it is difficult to think Jonson is not being ironical:

> Hath the proud Tiran, Frost, usurp'd the seate
> Of former beauty in my Loves faire cheek;
> Staining the roseat tincture of her blood,
> With the dull die of blew-congealing cold?
> No, sure the weather dares not so presume
> To hurt an object of her brightnesse. . . .[27]

Language of this kind, if it were possible in Jonson's maturity, would have been clearly ridiculed in the following dialogue. Audrey merely says, "I have heard much o' your words, but not o' your deeds." The rhetorical nature of the speech is recognized, but it is not made laughable to the audience.

The popular appeal of Jonson's next play, *The Case Is Altered*,[28] was due to the widespread interest in language. Nashe's reference early in 1599 to "the merry coblers cutte in that witty Play of *The Case is Altered*" [29] suggests the reason for the popular success of the play. Jonson makes affected speech the principal dramatic element of the entire subplot, and the characteristic speech of two distinct characters, Juniper and Onion. Juniper's language finds a close parallel in one speech of Ralph in the *Cobbler's Prophesie*, and in a whole scene of Strumbo in *Locrine*,[30] but Jonson extended the use of such speech throughout a play, and with variations made it the mark of more than one character. The interest of the subplot in *The Case Is Altered* is dependent not so much on action as on the character of Juniper, which is represented by his affectations of speech. The gusto with which he uses words makes him an object of sympathetic interest to the audience. His words have no precise meaning even as they appear to him; he is con-

[27] *Ibid.*, II, iv, 52–57 (III, 37).

[28] Though first published in 1609, this play is dated 1597–98 (Herford and Simpson, I, 306).

[29] *Lenten Stuffe*, in *The Works of Thomas Nashe*, ed. Ronald B. McKerrow (5 vols., London, 1904–10), III, 220.

[30] Baskervill pointed out these parallels (*English Elements*, p. 98).

tent with sound alone.[31] Nor are other dramatic characters persuaded that they mean anything, except sometimes Onion. But although Onion is a simple and pretentious type of gull, his gulling is not accomplished by Juniper's speech.[32]

The place of gulling in Jonson's early plays is to be observed because it is through this art that rhetorical speech later affects dramatic action. The dramatic possibilities of such hypocritical affectation seemed just beyond Jonson's view in *A Tale of a Tub*. Recognition seems nearer in *The Case Is Altered*. Valentine is a more sophisticated character than either Juniper or Onion, and when Juniper demands that he "discourse," Valentine begins: "(Now will I gull these ganders rarely:) Gentlemen hauing in my peregrination through Mesopotamia."[33] This speech has, in the light of Jonson's later plays, obvious dramatic possibilities, but it is interrupted here. In this play rhetorical speech remains principally a mark of character.

The response of the audience to the quality of Juniper's speech is guided by the comments of other characters. Valentine acts as a foil and commentator, a part which becomes more important in Jonson's plays as the rhetorical language becomes more elaborate. When Juniper asks him, "What *fortuna de la Guerra?*" Valentine remarks in an aside, "O how pittifully are these words forc't. As though they were pumpt out on's belly,"[34] and the wanted response of the audience is made explicit. When Jonson felt the need in other scenes for such a critical comment, he sometimes gave the words inappropriately to the simple and naïve Onion. "Ile be hangd & he were not misbegotten of some fencer,"[35] Onion remarks after Juniper has used a series of fencing terms. On occasion, however, Jonson

---

[31] "Meane? Gods so, ist not a good word man? what? stand vpon meaning with your friends? Puh, *Absconde*" (*The Case Is Altered*, I, iv, 9–10; Herford and Simpson, III, 110).

[32] He is "*Cupids* gull," according to Juniper (*The Case Is Altered*, IV, v, 15; Herford and Simpson, III, 156), and Onion later exclaims, "O conni-catching *Cupid*" (IV, vii, 52; Herford and Simpson, III, 160).

[33] *The Case Is Altered*, V, vi, 50–51 (III, 175).

[34] *Ibid.*, I, iv, 17–19 (III, 110).   [35] *Ibid.*, II, vii, 9–10 (III, 135).

was able, with dramatic effectiveness, to make Onion's criticism at once wise and appropriately naïve. When Juniper addresses Rachel for him and asks her, ". . . you smell my meaning?" Onion reflects, ". . . smell? O most odious . . . Filthy, by this finger! smell? smell a rat, smel a pudding. . . ." [36] But his comments were not always so fitting, and Jonson must have felt the need for a character whose entire function is critical. He was to create such characters in his "comical satires."

H. C. Hart finds the "light comedy between Juniper, Onion, and Valentine" so agreeable that he regrets Jonson's not cultivating it "instead of putting it aside." [37] It is true that Jonson does not again write comedy of this tone, but instead of putting aside its technique of using affected speech for dramatic purposes, he seems to have expanded it, gradually making greater demands on the literary sophistication of his audience.

In the group of plays which followed, *Every Man in His Humor* (1598), *Every Man Out of His Humor* (1599), *Cynthia's Revels* (1600), *Poetaster* (1601), Jonson introduces a variety of experiments, and his own estimate of them is suggested by the fact that these are the earliest plays he printed in his *Works*, published in 1616. In all of them Jonson continued to use affected speech as a mark of character, but he uses it with more subtlety and with more serious satirical purpose than he had done in *A Tale of a Tub* or *The Case Is Altered*. Although the vain affectations which exhibit character are predominant, deliberate affectations which are a means of persuasion become increasingly important. They not only exhibit character, but forward the action of the play.

In both versions of *Every Man in His Humor* affected speech is important, but it is highly characteristic of the revision that affectations are intensified, and specialized terms added. Some of the characteristics of Jonson's early affected language appear

---

[36] *Ibid.*, IV, vii, 32–38 (III, 160).
[37] *Notes and Queries*, 9th ser., XI (1903), 501.

only in the original version, which was published in 1601. For example, the following speech of Bobadilla to Stephano is as meaningless as Juniper's address to Maximilian in behalf of Onion:

Signior, I must tell you this, I am no generall man, embrace it as a most high fauour, for (by the host of Egypt) but that I conceiue you, to be a Gentleman of some parts. I loue few words: you haue wit: imagine.[38]

The development of Jonson's intention is suggested by comparing this with the complete clarity of the Folio version:

Sir, I must tell you this, I am no generall man, but for Mr. WEL-BRED's sake (you may embrace it, at what height of fauour you please) I doe communicate with you: and conceiue you, to bee a gentleman of some parts, I loue few wordes.[39]

Such nonsense even in the Quarto, however, is exceptional. Its want of meaning is not due like Juniper's to the misuse of words, but to a confused syntax, which was a convenient affectation of the ignorant ("you have wit: imagine"). As Jonson's art matured it tended to exclude language that was absolute nonsense. Instead of malapropisms and completely misunderstood words, Bobadill generally uses literary or technical terms with a fastidious accuracy. He understands the words he uses better than Juniper, but his understanding is superficial; it often proves to be limited to words. In place of the language of Juniper, Jonson was creating a dramatic speech which represented less obvious but more common and more significant errors in men's speech: the confusion between words and things.

The difference between the effect of Bobadill's speech and that of Juniper is also partly accounted for by their different stations in the social scale. As a professional soldier, Bobadill commands more respect from his associates than Juniper or Onion, and has larger pretensions. Because of his position the

[38] *Every Man in His Humor*, Quarto of 1601, II, iii, 72–75 (III, 228). Compare *The Case Is Altered*, I, viii, 1–10 (III, 118–19).
[39] *Every Man in His Humor*, Folio of 1616, III, i, 80–84 (III, 340).

response of the audience is less sympathetic to his affectations.
Like Juniper he belongs to a class of characters who had already
been represented on the English stage to some extent by their
affected speech. Crackstone in *Two Italian Gentlemen*, Basi-
lisco in *Soliman and Perseda*, and Bragadino in *The Blind Beggar
of Alexandria* have in common with Bobadill characteristics of
the *miles gloriosus*, but their affectations of speech are much
simpler. When Pedant comments on Crackstone's speech that
"He rowles in his Retorike as an Ape in his tayle," [40] his
physical and external metaphor suggests the difference between
the conventional affectations of these characters, and Bobadill's,
whose speech is so deeply a part of his character.

In *The Case Is Altered*, Juniper boasts his knowledge of the
"phrases" of the "mistery of the noble science" of defense, but
the dramatic possibilities of such a rhetorical display were not
tried until Jonson created Bobadill. Many of these affected
terms are found in the Quarto, but more are added in the Folio
revision:

> Bob[ADILL]. By the foot of Pharaoh, and't were my case now,
> I should send him a *chartel*, presently. The *bastinado!* A most
> proper, and sufficient *dependance*, warranted by the great Ca-
> ranza. Come hither. You shall *chartel* him. I'll shew you a trick,
> or two, you shall kill him with, at pleasure: the first *stoccata*, if
> you will, by this ayre.
> Mat[THEW]. Indeed, you haue absolute knowledge i' the mys-
> terie, I haue heard, sir.[41]

In the Quarto "bastinado" and "stockado" are found, but here,
in the Folio version, their effect is brought into clearer focus by
such changes as "chartel," both as noun and verb, for "chal-
lenge," and the addition of Carranza's authority for a "proper,
and sufficient *dependance*." In revision Jonson consistently
elaborates the kind of language which the audience is made to

[40] *Fidele and Fortunio, the Two Italian Gentlemen* (Stationers' Register,
1584, Malone Society Reprints, 1909), l. 1442.
[41] *Every Man in His Humor*, Folio of 1616, I, v, 110–17 (III, 321).

recognize as jargon.[42] The terms as such have been studied by Bobadill, and he tries, without being fully aware of his pretense, to pass them off to represent real knowledge. They are sheer rhetoric, however, and the strict limitation of Bobadill's knowledge appears when, trying to instruct Matthew in the skill, he carefully evades a trial in practice:

BOB. . . . So, indifferent. Hollow your body more sir, thus. Now, stand fast o' your left leg, note your distance, keepe your due proportion of time— Oh, you disorder your point, most irregularly!

MAT. How is the bearing of it, now, sir?

BOB. O, out of measure ill! A well-experienc'd hand would passe vpon you, at pleasure.

MAT. How meane you, sir, passe vpon me?

BOB. Why, thus sir (make a thrust at me) come in, vpon the answere, controll your point, and make a full carreere, at the body. The best-practis'd gallants of the time, name it the *passada:* a most desperate thrust, beleeue it!

MAT. Well, come, sir.

BOB. Why, you doe not manage your weapon with any facilitie, or grace to inuite mee: I haue no spirit to play with you. Your dearth of iudgement renders you tedious.

MAT. But one *venue,* sir.

BOB. *Venue!* Fie. Most grosse denomination, as euer I heard. O, the *stoccata,* while you liue, sir.[43]

This, the Folio version, is scarcely changed from the Quarto. The French "*venue,*" which Bobadill scorns in comparison with the Italian term, was commonly used in English, and had been assimilated to "veny" or "veney," the forms which appear in the Quarto. Jonson has given life to the conventional cowardice of the boastful soldier by making him hide his cowardice, perhaps even from himself, behind the screen of words.

[42] Compare the Quarto reading, "Hostesse, lend vs another bedstaffe here quickly: looke you sir, . . ." (I, iii, 195–96; Herford and Simpson, III, 212), with the Folio, "Hostesse, accommodate vs with another bed-staffe here, quickly: Lend vs another bed-staffe. The woman do's not vnderstand the wordes of *Action*. Looke you, sir" (I, v, 125–28; Herford and Simpson, III, 321).

[43] *Every Man in His Humor,* Folio of 1616, I, v, 133–51 (III, 321–22).

When Bobadill describes his plan for defeating an army of forty thousand with twenty men, he uses terms of fencing in affected rhetorical amplification: ". . . I would teach these nineteene, the speciall rules, as your *Punto*, your *Reuerso*, your *Stoccata*, your *Imbroccata*, your *Passada*, your *Montanto*: till they could all play very neare, or altogether as well as my selfe." [44] This language is intimately related to Bobadill's character. He is consciously exploiting its rhetorical value, but he is not able himself to use the language without being moved by it. He is gulled in a sense by his own speech; he is capable of being persuaded by his own rhetoric. After the disgraceful encounter with Downright, when he meets Matthew, his words are not directed to Matthew so much as to himself:

MAT. I, but would any man haue offered it in *Venice?* as you say?

BOB. Tut, I assure you, no: you shall haue there your *Nobilis*, your *Gentelezza*, come in brauely vpon your *reuerse*, stand you close, stand you firme, stand you faire, saue your *retricato* with his left legge, come to the *assalto* with the right, thrust with braue steele, defie your base wood! But, wherefore doe I awake this remembrance? I was fascinated, by IVPITER: fascinated: but I will be vn-witch'd, and reueng'd, by law.[45]

He seems to lose himself in a world of Italian words. It is here, moved by his own catalogue of terms used rhetorically, that he is really bewitched and fascinated.

In *Every Man Out of His Humor* and the other "comical satires," *Cynthia's Revels* and *Poetaster*, Jonson develops a dramatic technique in which characters are presented before a presumably critical audience like pictures at an exhibition.[46] Action and dialogue are often preceded by descriptions which prepare the audience to watch the presentation with superior knowledge. The literary quality of the speech of Fastidious

[44] *Ibid.*, IV, vii, 76–80 (III, 377). The Quarto has the same terms.
[45] *Ibid.*, IV, 9, 10–19 (III, 384–85).
[46] O. J. Campbell observes the similarity of this method to the method of formal satire (*Comicall Satyre and Shakespeare's Troilus and Cressida*, San Marino, Calif., 1938, p. 79).

Brisk in *Every Man Out of His Humor* is an important device for exhibiting the character of this *"neat, spruce, affecting Courtier."* [47] His description of life at court illustrates the brilliance which Jonson was now capable of giving to affected speech.

A man liues there, in that diuine rapture, that hee will thinke himselfe i' the ninth heauen for the time, and lose all sense of mortalitie whatsoeuer; when he shall behold such glorious (and almost immortall) beauties, heare such angelicall and harmonious voyces, discourse with such flowing and *ambrosian* spirits, whose wits are as suddaine as lightning, and humorous as *nectar;* Oh: it makes a man al *quintessence*, and *flame* & lifts him vp (in a moment) to the verie christall crowne of the skie, where (houering in the strength of his imagination) he shall behold all the delights of the HESPERIDES, the *Insulæ Fortunatæ*, ADONIS gardens, *Tempe* or what else (confin'd within the amplest verge of *poesie*) to bee meere *vmbræ*, and imperfect figures, conferr'd with the most essentiall felicitie of your court. [48]

Language of this kind requires a more alert, critical response than the barbarities of Juniper's speech, or the relatively simple affectations of Bobadill. Macilente's comment guides the reaction of the audience: "Well, this *Encomion* was not extemporall, it came too perfectly off." The speech of Fastidious is self-conscious and studied, but it is still an affectation of vanity. His speech, like Bobadill's, is deeply rooted in his character. Dramatic action in the "comical satires" is subordinated to rhetorical exhibition of this kind.

In writing a piece of personal satire against Marston in *Poetaster*, Jonson used the methods he had been developing, and like Nashe when he quarreled with Harvey, ridiculed the speech of his opponent, identifying it with the affected jargon of Crispinus. In the early scenes of the play Crispinus's diction is inappropriate and affected. Even to the simple citizen Albius, he speaks affectedly: ". . . you are most delicately seated

[47] *Every Man Out of His Humor*, "The Character of the Persons" (III, 424).
[48] *Ibid.*, IV, 8, 18-32 (III, 556-57).

here . . ." and later, "I am most strenuously well, I thanke you, sir."[49] When he lays hold upon Horace his speech has the same quality, and it includes some special terms of various branches of learning with which he affects to be acquainted:

By PHŒBVS, here's a most neate fine street, is't not? I protest to thee, I am enamour'd of this street now, more then of halfe the streets of *Rome*, againe; 'tis so polite, and terse! There's the front of a building now. I studie architecture too: if euer I should build, I'de haue a house of iust that *prospectiue*.[50]

Suddenly, but characteristically, he changes the subject from architecture to poetry, then to hairdressing:

I cannot tell, but it stirres me more then all your court-curles, or your spangles, or your tricks: I affect not these high gable-ends, these *tuscane*-tops, nor your coronets, nor your arches, nor your *pyramid's;* giue me a fine sweet—little delicate dressing, with a bodkin, as you say: and a mushrome, for all your other ornatures.[51]

Jonson notes his indebtedness to a Satire of Horace for this scene, but the peculiar quality of Crispinus's speech is not borrowed. Horace had merely said that the bore "rattled on about everything, praising the streets and the city."[52] Jonson had already created a dramatic speech appropriate to such a character, and he uses it here. Jonson's Horace is quite helpless against the "worded trash" of the ignorant, as later, in different situations, Volpone, Morose, and Subtle will be. This scene in effect is not unlike those in *Volpone* and *Epicoene* for which Jonson was indebted to Libanius.

The personal satire against Marston is most explicit in the last act when Crispinus's verses, which are read before the court, are largely composed of Marston's words. To a reader of *The Scourge of Villainy*, they must have seemed a cogent parody not only of Marston's strange diction, but of his verse

---

[49] *Poetaster*, II, i, 4–5, 13 (IV, 220–21).   [50] *Ibid.*, III, i, 30–35 (IV, 234–35).
[51] *Ibid.*, III, i, 50–55 (IV, 235).
[52] ". . . cum quidlibet ille garriret, vicos, urbem landaret" (Horace's *Satires*, I, ix, 12–13, Loeb Classical Library, p. 105).

rhythms too. The fact that some words which are ridiculed are
not found in Marston is probably due to an expedient revision
of *What You Will*, which seems to have been produced before
Poetaster,[53] though not published until 1607. Jonson showed
complete scorn for Marston by identifying him with such
types of ignorance and folly as he had already represented on the
stage. When Virgil admonishes Crispinus, he expresses Jonson's
attitude toward all kinds of jargon:

> You must not hunt for wild, out-landish termes,
> To stuffe out a peculiar *dialect*;
> But let your *matter* runne before your *words*: . . .[54]

In the final scene of *Poetaster*, however, jargon is not really used
as dramatic speech at all. Crispinus's poem is read only as evidence in a court trial, and the purge of "out-landish termes,"
which Jonson imitated from Lucian, is mere allegory.

Bobadill, Brisk, and Crispinus use language which clearly received greater attention from Jonson than the simple language
of gulls, who merely try to ape their superiors. These characters
are not to be considered gulls.[55] Their speech, though vainly
affected, is often rich in invention, and their art not despicable.
Their characters are revealed by their speech,[56] but their manner of speaking has little effect on the action of the play. As impostors, they are in a sense prototypes of Volpone and Subtle,
but unlike these later characters their language is not a tool
which they consciously manipulate. If on rare occasion their
language happens to influence the actions of other characters,
it is the result of coincidence, rather than consciously applied
purpose.

[53] R. A. Small, *The Stage-Quarrel* (Breslau, 1899), pp. 101–14.

[54] *Poetaster*, V, iii, 549–51 (IV, 314).

[55] In the Quarto of *Every Man in His Humor* (I, i, 155; Herford and Simpson, III, 201), Prospero describes Bobadilla with Mattheo as a gull, but this
passage is omitted in the Folio.

[56] Of language Jonson wrote, translating from Vives: "It springs out of the
most retired, and inmost parts of us, and is the Image of the Parent of it, the
mind" (*Discoveries*, in *Ben Jonson*, ed. Herford and Simpson, VIII, 625).

There are some characters in the early plays, however, who use language deliberately in rhetorical persuasion. The situations which they create are comparable to situations developed in later plays. Some of these characters have an ironic view of other characters which they share with the audience. In *Every Man in His Humor*, Edward Knowell and Wellbred sometimes adapt their speech to the style that will impress Stephen, a would-be gentleman. Edward Knowell uses an affected literary style to persuade his cousin to appear more proud and melancholy. It appears in the Quarto, but is more firmly drawn in the Folio by further exaggeration:

Come, wrong not the qualitie of your desert, with looking downeward, couz; but hold vp your head, so: and let the *Idea* of what you are, be pourtray'd i' your face, that men may reade i' your physnomie, (*Here, within this place, is to be seene the true, rare, and accomplish'd monster, or miracle of nature,* which is all one.) [57]

Similarly when Wellbred first meets Stephen he addresses him ironically in a gallant's phrase: "I know not your name sir, but I shall be glad of any occasion, to render me more familiar to you." [58] The motive of Edward Knowell and Wellbred is only to expose folly and ignorance. By their use of exaggerated language they encourage the foolish characters to display their humors, and are thus presenters of the action, not hypocrites.

Brainworm, on the other hand, uses deliberate affectations of speech in order to further his own ends. Although in his disguises he does not show the brilliant rhetorical skill which is to be used in later plays, he uses place names as a professional jargon when he masquerades as a soldier: "I was twice shot at the taking of *Alepo*, once at the reliefe of *Vienna;* I have beene at *Marseilles, Naples,* and the *Adriatique* gulfe." [59] Jonson seems to be increasingly aware, even in the Quarto version, of the dramatic possibilities of such speech as Brainworm uses when he

[57] *Every Man in His Humor*, Folio of 1616, I, iii, 122–27 (III, 314).
[58] *Ibid.*, III, i, 73–75 (III, 340).   [59] *Ibid.*, II, iv, 62–64 (III, 332).

is in disguise. In the Quarto Prospero (Wellbred) and Lorenzo Junior (Edward Knowell) comment on his speech:

> PROS[PERO]. Why Musco: who would haue thought thou hadst beene such a gallant?
> Lo[RENZO] IU[NIOR]. I cannot tell, but (vnles a man had iuggled begging all his life time, and beene a weauer of phrases from his infancie, for the apparrelling of it) I thinke the world cannot produce his Riuall.[60]

But in the Folio revision a greater emphasis is put upon studied artistry:

> WEL[L-BRED]. Why, BRAYNE-WORME, who would haue thought thou hadst beene such an artificer?
> E[D]. KN[O'WELL]. An artificer! An architect! except a man had studied begging all his life-time, and beene a weauer of language, from his infancie, for the clothing of it! I neuer saw his riuall.[61]

Brainworm may seem not to live up to this high praise, but it clearly indicates Jonson's intention to create a conscious manipulator of language capable of influencing other characters, and through them, the course of the action. He seems to have become more conscious of this purpose at the time of revision.[62]

Among these earlier plays, the most extended use of the device for this effect is in the Folio version of *Cynthia's Revels*, the date of which unfortunately is not certain.[63] Mercury and Crites use a courtly jargon to gull the courtiers and expose their folly. More interesting still, especially if the Folio version is

---

[60] *Ibid.*, Quarto of 1601, III, ii, 23–28 (III, 239).

[61] *Ibid.*, Folio of 1616, III, v, 24–29 (III, 353–54).

[62] In *Every Man Out of His Humor*, Shift, as a professor of the use of tobacco and as a soldier, uses language with a similar motive and similar effect (III, iii, 47–59; III, vi, 51–57; Herford and Simpson, III, 500–501, 509–10). Clove also, in a single scene, accumulates terms to "make 'hem beleeue we are great schollers" (III, iv, 6–30; Herford and Simpson, III, 502–503).

[63] Baskervill thinks "that the longer form was the original form" (*English Elements*, p. 227); Herford and Simpson say, "The Folio text of 1616 is a revision and expansion of the Quarto," but they add that in revising Jonson probably drew upon a longer version than the Quarto, which he had kept in manuscript since the date of original composition (IV, 17).

actually earlier than the Quarto, is the use of vocational jargon by the tradesmen with whom Amorphus and Mercury deal in the middle of the courting contest. In the scene in which Amorphus meets his perfumer in preparation for the second half of his courting duel, he speaks in character by affecting a technical term. "I sauour no *sampsuchine*, in it." [64] But the situation is different from the others in which he affectedly displays his knowledge. It is changed by the presence of the perfumer, whose knowledge of his trade gives him confidence before such a pretender as Amorphus. He feels he can afford to be candid: "Ile tell you all the ingredients, sir." Amorphus continues to consider himself the perfumer's equal in such knowledge, and puns on another technical term:

AMO[RPHVS]. You shall be simple, to discouer your *simples*.
PER[FUMER]. Simple? why sir? what recke I to whom I discouer? I haue in it, *muske, ciuet, amber, phœnicobalanus*, the decoction of *turmericke, sesama, nard, spikenard, calamus odoratus, stacte, opobalsamum, amomum, storax, ladanum, aspalathum, opoponax, oenanthe*. And what of all these now? what are you the better? Tut, it is the sorting, and the diuiding, and the mixing, and the tempring, and the searcing, and the decocting, that makes the fumigation, and the suffumigation. [65]

Such an accumulation of professional terms for rhetorical purposes is characteristic of Jonson's mature style. The perfumer has succeeded in asserting his authority, and has exposed Amorphus's pretense.

AMO. Well, indue me with it.
PER. I will, sir.

But Amorphus has only learned the practical lesson of not questioning the perfumer too far. Later in the scene when he is offered "an excellent *diapasme* in a chaine," he says:

AMO. Stay, what are the ingredients to your *fucus?*
PER. Nought, but *sublimate*, and *crude mercurie*, sir, well pre-

[64] *Cynthia's Revels*, V, iv, 314 (IV, 148).
[65] *Ibid.*, V, iv, 318-27 (IV, 148-49).

par'd, and dulcified, with the jaw-bones of a sow, burnt, beaten, and searced.

AMO. I approue it. Lay it on.[66]

It is difficult to believe that this was written in 1600. The vigorous use of jargon suggests a date nearer that of *The Alchemist*.

Mercury and Crites have no jargon of their own, but they cultivate that of the courtiers in a plot to gull them and expose their folly. As Mercury says to Cupid, "Since wee are turn'd cracks, let's studie to be like cracks; practice their language, . . . and not vtter a phrase, but what shall come forth steept in the verie brine of conceipt, and sparkle like salt in fire." [67] And later, before the contest, Mercury says, "Well, I haue a plot vpon these prizers, for which, I must presently find out CRITES, and with his assistance, pursue it to a high straine of laughter, or MERCVRIE hath lost of his mettall." [68] Appearing at the contest, they force Amorphus to accept Mercury as a challenger at "the foure choice, and principall weapons" of the "subtile science of *Courtship*." These "weapons" are given names which form part of a special technical vocabulary for courtiers: "the *bare Accost*, the *better Regard*, the *solemne Addresse*, and the *perfect Close*." [69] Each one is composed of a set form of speech, the component parts of which were studied and named also. The first requires no words. After Mercury's formal bow, Phantaste comments, "Sprightly, and short," and Anaides knowingly agrees, calling it by its precise name: "True, it is the *french curteau*." [70] Crites joins ironically in the naming of every trifling movement: ". . . worthily studied. This is th' *exalted Fore-top*, . . . This is call'd the *solemne band-string*, . . . this is y'cleped the *serious trifle*." And in an aside to the audience he asks, ". . . would any reasonable creature make these his serious studies, and perfections? Much lesse, onely liue to these ends?" [71] In the second "weapon" words are used, for as

[66] *Ibid.*, V, iv, 402–406 (IV, 151).   [67] *Ibid.*, II, i, 4–10 (IV, 63).

[68] *Ibid.*, IV, v, 148–51 (IV, 130).   [69] *Ibid.*, IV, v, 98–99 (IV, 129).

[70] *Ibid.*, V, iv, 152 (IV, 143).   [71] *Ibid.*, V, iv, 147–76 (IV, 143–44).

Asotus explains, "how should it bee the *better Reguard*, else?"
In the presentation of compliments, Mercury's sarcasm is un-
appreciated, and when he is actually awarded a prize, Crites
says, ". . . you should doe more charitably, to doe it more
openly; that they might discouer themselues mockt in these
monstrous affections." [72] In the "solemne Addresse," therefore,
Mercury speaks with more exaggerated affectation,[73] and his
irony, though still not understood by the courtiers, is obvious to
the audience. Unlike the language of a character like Fastidious
Brisk, which it resembles in form, its irony is directly implied
by the person speaking. The speech of Fastidious Brisk is understood ironically by the audience only. Mercury is himself an
ironist. His speech acquires a dramatic interest from the failure
of the courtiers to appreciate its real meaning. Like Mercury in
this scene, Volpone and Subtle, in Jonson's later comedies, are
ironists, but they are at the same time, like Fastidious, impostors. They have a personal interest in being misunderstood,
and, consequently, when their deliberately affected language
is used in rhetorical persuasion and is misunderstood, it has a
greater effect of dramatic irony than Mercury's. The irony of
Mercury, which is to a certain extent undramatic, thus forms a
transitional link between the comic irony of the early and of
the later plays.

The courtiers fail to understand the ridicule being heaped on
them until Crites challenges Anaides. He decides to anticipate
Anaides in everything, and "leaue him not so much as a looke,
an eye, a stalke, or an imperfect oth, to expresse himselfe by,
after me." [74] His speech is a parody which Hedon and the rest
can understand:

. . . which is the *Peece*, stands forth to bee courted? O, are you
shee? Well, Madame, or sweet lady, it is so, I doe loue you in some
sort, doe you conceiue? and though I am no *Monsieur*, nor no
Signior, and do want (as they say) *logicke* and *sophistrie*, and good

[72] *Ibid.*, V, iv, 288–90 (IV, 147).   [73] *Ibid.*, V, iv, 429–36 (IV, 152).
[74] *Ibid.*, V, iv, 573–74 (IV, 156).

words, to tell you why it is so; yet by this hand, and by that candle, it is so; And though I bee no booke-worme, nor one that deales by arte, to giue you *rhetorike*, and causes, why it should be so, or make it good it is so, yet dam' me, but I know it is so, and am assur'd it is so, and I and my sword shall make it appeare it is so; and giue you reason sufficient, how it can be no otherwise, but so—— [75]

The accumulation of clichés and the ignorant logic of this speech are obvious even to the stage audience. The bluntness of its satire, in contrast with Mercury's, is dictated ironically by the needs of the courtiers to whom it is indirectly addressed.

Most jargon in the early plays of Jonson is the language of the affected Elizabethan gentleman, or the person who would imitate him. It ranges from the lightly satirical imitation in Juniper's speech in *The Case Is Altered* to the brilliant, affected refinement of the speech of Fastidious Brisk. The trend of Jonson's development is indicated in the plays before *Sejanus* by the increasingly large infusion of technical terms. In *Every Man in His Humor*, there are many terms of fencing, tobacco-taking, and the military profession. In *Cynthia's Revels* the language of the perfumer's shop is prominent as well as a large number of special terms used by Amorphus to advertise his knowledge of literature,[76] music,[77] fencing,[78] and heraldry,[79] all subjects worthy of a gentleman's study. In *Poetaster*, the jargon of the legal profession is contrasted with the pure style cultivated by Ovid Junior.[80] The inkhorn terms of the professional writer are satirized directly in the personal attack upon Marston.

---

[75] *Ibid.*, V, iv, 577–88 (IV, 156).

[76] "I am neither your *Minotaure*, nor your *Centaure*, nor your *Satyre*, nor your *Hyæna*, nor your *Babion* . . ." (*Cynthia's Revels*, I, iii, 4–5; Herford and Simpson, IV, 52).

[77] ". . . you see how I doe enter with an odde *minnum*, and driue it thorow the *briefe* . . ." (*Ibid.*, IV, iii, 331–32; Herford and Simpson, IV, 119).

[78] ". . . you haue your *passages*, and *imbroccata's* in *courtship*; as the *bitter Bob* in wit; the *Reuerse* in face, or wry-mouth" (*Ibid.*, V, ii, 63–65; Herford and Simpson, IV, 134).

[79] *Ibid.*, III, v, 72–83 (IV, 96).   [80] *Poetaster*, I, ii, 105–107 (IV, 212).

The increasing use of the language of all "professors" is a marked tendency in the growth of Jonson's dramatic speech. The strange words, the clichés, and the special terms used in the early plays represent pretenses to polite learning. The pretenses of the learned "professors," each with a technical vocabulary of his own, are of greater interest to Jonson in his later plays. The dominant types in the early plays, the gentleman or would-be gentleman and his zany, are replaced later by the knave and his gull. But the knave also inherits, to a large degree, the role of the critic in earlier plays, and he is often himself an ironist as well as a hypocrite.

The dramatic effect of jargon in the early plays depends little upon action. It is used to delineate several types of characters, whose speech the audience can observe with an ironist's superiority of knowledge and judgment. Language influences the dramatic action, however, when it is affected as a means of deception or persuasion. It is so used by the "professors," who begin to appear in the early plays. The self-conscious and often ironical hypocrite who manipulates such language to "betray that way" becomes the Jonsonian hero.

CHAPTER V

JARGON AS DRAMATIC SPEECH IN JONSON'S MATURITY

T HE RHETORICAL language of special "terms," which Jonson elaborated in his early plays and used principally as a satirical mark of character, becomes in his dramatic maturity a technique which produces a variety of ironic effects. Jargon is spoken most frequently by knaves with a conscious purpose of persuasion, and is imitated by fools. As dramatic speech, it not only represents character, but also is a means of forwarding the plot and of emphasizing the irony of a situation which the plot presents.

In *Sejanus* (1603), Jonson introduces professional jargon in certain scenes with an effect different from anything found in his earlier plays. Though he was conscious of writing a tragedy, the effect of these scenes is not unlike that of his mature comedies. Their effect is comic and results from the peculiar ironic light which the language, technical jargon particularly, casts on the dramatic situation. The speech of Eudemus, the physician, is especially characterized by jargon. The rhetorical nature of his speech is recognized by Sejanus. When Eudemus promises to help Sejanus's suit to Livia, the wife of Drusus, his words are so comforting that Sejanus exclaims in soliloquy:

> Let me adore my ÆSCVLAPIVS.
> Why, this indeed is physick! and out-speakes
> The knowledge of cheape drugs, or any vse
> Can be made out of it! more comforting
> Then all your *opiates, iulebes, apozemes,*
> Magistrall *syrrupes*. . . .[1]

[1] *Sejanus,* I, 355–60 (*Ben Jonson,* ed. C. H. Herford, Percy and Evelyn Simpson, 10 vols., Oxford, 1925– , IV, 367). All references to Jonson's plays are to this edition. Volume and page are given in parentheses, immediately following the citation.

"Out-speakes" is an appropriate word, because Sejanus implies throughout that the comforts of physicians, like this of Eudemus, are due principally to speech. But the speech of physicians, composed out of "the knowledge of cheape drugs," is merely rhetorical. That of Eudemus promises more real comfort, and therefore "indeed is physick." Spoken in soliloquy, the technical terms are not calculated to affect other dramatic characters, but in the mind of the audience they amplify the effect of "cheape drugs." The satire against professional rhetoric is here merely incidental to Jonson's dramatic purpose.

When Eudemus meets Livia on a professional visit he uses the occasion to further Sejanus's plot. The terms of cosmetics [2] have great dramatic value in pointing the contrasts between appearance and reality:

EVD.   SEIANVS, for your loue! his very name
        Commandeth aboue CVPID, or his shafts—
(LIV.   Nay, now yo' haue made it worse.
EVD.   I'le helpe it straight.)
        And, but pronounc'd, is a sufficient charme
        Against all rumour; and of absolute power
        To satisfie for any ladies honour.
(LIV.   What doe you now, EVDEMVS?
EVD.   Make a light *fucus*,
        To touch you ore withall.) Honor'd SEIANVS!
        What act (though ne're so strange, and insolent)
        But that addition will at least beare out,
        If't doe not expiate?
LIV.   Here, good physitian.
EVD.   I like this studie to preserue the loue
        Of such a man, that comes not euery houre
        To greet the world. ('Tis now well, ladie, you should
        Vse of the *dentifrice*, I prescrib'd you, too,

---

[2] Perfume and terms of cosmetics are used metaphorically by the satirists. Marston writes:

      Perfume this nastie age, smugge *Lesbia*
      Hath stinking lunges, although a simpring grace,
      A muddy inside, though a surphul'd face
         (*Scourge of Villanie*, Bk. I, Sat. 1, ed. G. B. Harrison, London and New York, 1925, p. 16).

> To cleere your teeth, and the prepar'd *pomatum*,
> To smoothe the skin:) . . .[3]

The world of appearance is that of "Cvpid," "honour," "loue," "such a man, that comes not euery houre To greet the world." Livia's unclean teeth and unsmooth skin are a reality. The real political motives of Sejanus are hidden by Eudemus's words, and the real Livia is hidden behind the outward show of cosmetics. The terms of cosmetics give a strong sense of the artificial concealment of the truth. They are used not for their effect on Livia (she seems hardly aware of them), but to intensify the spectator's sense of irony.

The contrasts between appearance and reality are continued throughout the scene. Eudemus praises Livia for betraying her husband: "The ages that succeed . . . shall admire And reckon it an act, without your sexe: It hath that rare apparance." [4] Again, when Sejanus takes his leave, Livia expresses sententiously the desirability of concealment, and Eudemus again shocks the audience into a sense of the real:

> Liv.   The thoughts be best, are least set forth to shew.
> Evd.   When will you take some physick, lady?
> Liv.   When
>   I shall, Evdemvs: But let Drvsvs drug
>   Be first prepar'd.
> Evd.   Were Lygdvs made, that's done;
>   I haue it readie. And to morrow-morning,
>   I'le send you a perfume, first to resolue,
>   And procure sweat, and then prepare a bath
>   To clense, and cleere the *cutis;* against when,
>   I'le haue an excellent new *fucus* made,
>   Resistiue 'gainst the sunne, the raine, or wind,
>   Which you shall lay on with a breath, or oyle,
>   As you best like, and last some fourteene houres.[5]

The shock of the word "perfume" is obviously calculated, and it introduces a passage which to the audience is rich in irony.

[3] *Sejanus*, II, 65–81 (IV, 377).   [4] *Ibid.*, II, 91–94 (IV, 378).
[5] *Ibid.*, II, 120–31 (IV, 378–79).

With perfumes, baths, and the doctor's "excellent new *fucus*," Livia will be able to conceal, outwardly at least, her blackened character; such preservatives, the doctor boasts, will "last some fourteene houres." The poetic value of the terms of cosmetics in this scene can be appreciated if one tries to substitute simple nontechnical words for them. The result would be leveling down, as if metaphors were cut away.

In *Volpone* (1606) Jonson develops further the integration of rhetorical language with action. Like Brainworm and Shift, Volpone goes through a series of disguises, but this simple action is given more dramatic significance than in the earlier plays. His disguises also depend much more upon the use of language than those of Brainworm and Shift. The technical terms which he uses are drawn primarily from the medical sciences. Unlike those in *Sejanus*, however, they are not used as an indirect commentary on a dramatic situation, but to complete a disguise, thereby creating the dramatic situation itself. When Volpone disguises as a mountebank to appear before Celia's window, he is an impostor playing the role of an impostor. Imitating the language of mountebanks, "Made all of termes and shreds," Volpone delights in his success, for he is an ironist as well. Although his purpose was only to get a view of Celia, he makes a dupe in this scene of Sir Politic Wouldbe, a member of his stage audience. Volpone's speech of nearly two hundred lines before Celia appears has a dramatic interest because the audience listens to it as rhetoric and is able to watch its effect. The suit to Celia merely provides the occasion. In one part of Volpone's speech, the rhetoric is marked especially by the use of technical terms.

. . . '*tis this blessed* vnguento, *this rare extraction, that hath only power to disperse all malignant humours, that proceed, either of hot, cold, moist, or windy causes——* . . . *To fortifie the most indigest, and crude stomack, I, were it of one, that (through extreme weakenesse) vomited bloud, applying only a warme napkin to the place, after the* vnction, *and fricace; for the* vertigine, *in the head, putting but a drop into your nostrills, likewise, behind the eares; a most soueraigne, and approued remedie: the* mal-

caduco, *crampes, conuulsions, paralysies, epilepsies,* tremor-
cordia, *retyred-nerues, ill vapours of the spleene, stoppings of the
liuer, the stone, the strangury,* hernia ventosa, iliaca passio; *stops a*
disenteria, *immediately; easeth the torsion of the small guts; and
cures* melancolia hypocondriaca, *being taken and applyed, according to my printed receipt.*[6]

The medical terms represent real learning to Sir Politic, who
asks his friend Peregrine, "Is not his language rare?"[7] Peregrine's comment makes certain that the audience will understand the language as a rhetorical jargon. The jargons of the
alchemists and the Puritans, which Jonson was later to make so
much of, are mentioned by way of comparison:

> But *Alchimy,*
> I neuer heard the like: or BROVGHTONS bookes.[8]

Volpone's use of jargon looks forward to *The Alchemist,*
but Lady Wouldbe's language has parallels in the earlier as well
as the later plays. Like Crispinus in *Poetaster* she affects a broad
acquaintance with the polite learning of the time. Her speech
is composed of a literary affectation as well as the special terms
of various arts. The scene in which Volpone is tormented by
her "eternall tongue" was suggested to Jonson by a declamation of Libanius,[9] but the special language in which this situation is dramatized is Jonson's own invention. Indeed he may
have been attracted to the situation because the jargon which
he had been using in earlier plays was so appropriate to it. The
hounding of Horace by Crispinus in *Poetaster* utilized jargon
in a similar way to represent learning to a foolish character and
painful nonsense to an intelligent one. When Volpone pretends
to be ill in order to stop Lady Wouldbe's flood of words, he
brings down on himself a torrent of medical terms:

> Lad.   Alas, good soule! the passion of the heart.
>   Seed-pearle were good now, boild with syrrope of apples,
>   Tincture of gold, and corrall, citron-pills,

---

[6] *Volpone,* II, ii, 94–110 (V, 52–53).   [7] *Ibid.,* II, ii, 118 (V, 53).
[8] *Ibid.,* II, ii, 118–19 (V, 53).
[9] E. C. Baldwin, "Ben Jonson's Indebtedness to the Greek Character-
sketch," *Modern Language Notes,* XVI (1901), 196–97.

      Your elicampane roote, mirobalanes——
VOLP. Ay me, I haue tane a grasse-hopper by the wing.
LAD. Burnt silke, and amber, you haue muscadell
      Good i' the house—
VOLP.   You will not drinke, and part?
LAD. No, feare not that. I doubt, we shall not get
      Some *english* saffron (halfe a dram would serue)
      Your sixteene cloues, a little muske, dri'd mints,
      Buglosse, and barley-meale—
VOLP.   Shee's in againe,
      Before I fayn'd diseases, now I haue one.[10]

This accumulation of terms is bolder than in the earlier plays; Jonson seems to draw with a surer purpose, in heavy, firm lines. Lady Wouldbe's rhetoric is a caricature, but it does more than simply represent her character. Its meaning is enriched by the dramatic situation, and its quality as language contributes to the dramatic effect. Volpone is tortured by words which are without meaning, but he is responsible for his own torture. Since Lady Wouldbe is one of his clients, he has a strong motive for listening patiently to her.

There are close parallels in *Epicoene* (1609) to the encounter between Volpone and Lady Wouldbe. The speech of Sir John Daw, made up like Lady Wouldbe's of a jargon of literary names and medical terms, is drawn out by the presenting characters to torture Morose with its noise. Epicoene, with a knowledge of the quality of his speech and of Morose's weakness, invites Sir John as a reader of the medical authorities to speak some words of comfort for her sake:

EPI. . . . Seruant, you haue read PLINY, and PARACELSVS: Ne're a word now to comfort a poore gentlewoman? Ay me! what fortune had I to marry a distracted man?
    DAW. I'll tell you, mistris—

            . . .

The disease in *Greeke* is called Μανία, in *Latine, Insania, Furor, vel Ecstasis melancholica*, that is, *Egressio*, when a man *ex melancholico, euadit fanaticus.*
    MOR. Shall I haue a lecture read vpon me aliue?

[10] *Volpone*, III, iv, 51–62 (V, 72–73).

Daw. But he may be but *Phreneticus,* yet, mistris? and *Phrenetis* is only *delirium,* or so— [11]

Morose reacts as Volpone did to Lady Wouldbe's "worded trash," but the eccentricity of his character, his aversion to noise of any kind, weakens the satire on the language as such. The reasonableness of his response to Sir John Daw's nonsense, however, tends to make his character more credible and significant to the audience. The scene in *Epicoene* differs from that in *Volpone* because of the presence of a third character whose plot is responsible for the situation. The audience is thus made to share its detachment with a character on the stage, and its sense of irony is thereby increased.

In *Epicoene* Jonson has taken pains to prepare the audience for scenes of this kind. Sir John Daw's first appearance, to the amusement of other characters as well as the audience, is given to a display of his manner of speaking. This early scene has the dramatic interest of the Humor plays in which a character is ironically portrayed through his speech, but it serves also to prepare the audience to accept his speech as natural in the later scene with Morose, and to accept Morose's reaction to it as not unreasonable. Other examples of such preparation are found in this play. The speech of both Cutbeard and Otter is characterized by Latin tags. Clerimont comments at one point on Cutbeard's speech, "How the slaue doth *latine* it!" [12] And Truewit, in describing the character of Otter, says he "do's *latine* it as much as your barber." [13] This common characteristic of their speech is, of course, much illustrated in the dialogue. Its dramatic value, however, is not only that it represents the characters of these two men; if that were so it would seem strange that two quite different characters should have the same outstanding peculiarity of speech. This peculiarity is apparently given to both characters so that in the later scene, when they are disguised before Morose as a parson and a canon-lawyer respec-

[11] *Epicoene,* IV, iv, 61–73 (V, 231).   [12] *Ibid.,* II, vi, 26 (V, 197).
[13] *Ibid.,* II, vi, 53–54 (V, 198).

tively, their use of the Latin jargon of these professions will seem not unnatural to the audience.[14]

What serves as another preparation for the scene in which Morose visits Cutbeard and Otter is the speech of Morose upon returning from the law court where he had gone to seek advice about a divorce. Dauphine asks him whether he spoke to a lawyer:

> MOR. O, no! there is such a noyse i' the court, that they haue frighted mee home, with more violence then I went! such speaking, and counter-speaking, with their seuerall voyces of *citations, appellations, allegations, certificates, attachments, intergatories, references, conuictions,* and *afflictions* indeed, among the Doctors and Proctors! that the noise here is silence too 't! a kind of calme mid-night! [15]

This speech, indebted like others in this play to a declamation of Libanius, has a dramatic value here of preparing the audience to accept the scene of Morose's gulling by Cutbeard and Otter. When these ignorant characters in disguise use the Latin jargon of the ecclesiastical courts, Morose can perceive their ignorance, but he can make no distinction between them and real members of their professions. Their successful disguise is therefore partly accounted for by Morose's attitude toward lawyers' jargon, which the audience knows from this speech. The original of Morose, in the Latin translation of Libanius published in 1606, explains why he stays away from law courts:

> Nec forum valde frequēto, propter istaec multa litium nomina, delatio, accusatio, abductio, actio, prescriptio. Quae illi etiam quib. negotiũ nullum est, libenter in ore habēt.[16]

Jonson's Morose is a more subtle critic than his original, and his criticism is more acceptable to a thoughtful audience. Instead

---

[14] When Truewit plans the disguise, he recalls that "The Barber smatters *latin*," and Dauphine adds, "Yes, and OTTER too" (*Epicoene*, IV, vii, 50–52; Herford and Simpson, V, 250).

[15] *Epicoene*, IV, vii, 13–19 (V, 249).

[16] Quoted by Aurelia Henry, ed., *Epicoene*, in "Yale Studies in English," Vol. XXXI (New Haven, 1906), p. xxx.

of objecting merely to the use of legal names by persons without business in the court, Jonson's Morose objects to the "speaking and counterspeaking" of the lawyers themselves in prosecuting actual cases. The satire is again weakened somewhat by Morose's aversion to speaking of all kinds, whether jargon or not, but the satire on language is merely incidental to the play. The speech of Morose ridiculing the jargon of lawyers has the effect of giving his character more substance. It is a speech with which the audience is bound to sympathize, and Morose, for the moment at least, appears quite reasonable.

It is Truewit who offers to bring to Morose "a very sufficient lawyer, and a learned Diuine" to advise him on his divorce. He disguises Otter and Cutbeard in the clothes of a parson and a man of law; besides clothes, he says, one need only "giue 'hem a few termes i' their mouthes." [17] "Onely remember your termes," he tells them, "and you are safe. Let the matter goe where it will: you haue many will do so." [18] In the scene which follows, a language such as Morose previously described becomes dramatic speech. The audience has been prepared to accept the use of learned tags of speech by two ignorant characters, and also to understand the failure of Morose to detect their disguise. Morose, in welcoming his tormentors, explains his attitude "that it be not strange," and at the same time reviews for the audience a situation that is highly charged with potential irony. It is a moment of calm before the sparks begin to fly:

My father, in my education, was wont to aduise mee, that I should alwayes collect, and contayne my mind, not suffring it to flow loosely. . . . So that I come not to your publike pleadings, or your places of noise; not that I neglect those things, that make for the dignitie of the common-wealth: but for the meere auoiding of clamors, & impertinencies of Orators, that know not how to be silent. And for the cause of noise, am I now a sutor to you. . . .[19]

[17] *Epicoene*, IV, vii, 45 (V, 250).   [18] *Ibid.*, V, iii, 16–18 (V, 257).
[19] *Ibid.*, V, iii, 48–60 (V, 258).

Except for the last sentence this is a fairly close translation of the passage in Libanius which precedes the catalogue of names adapted by Jonson earlier in the play. The last sentence has a special point because it is "for the cause of noise" that Truewit has disguised and introduced Cutbeard and Otter. At first Morose patiently explains the reason for his attitude, and it is only gradually that his patience is worn down by the Latin-English jargon of the canon lawyer:

> CVT. Your question is, for how many causes a man may haue *diuortium legitimum*, a lawfull diuorce. First, you must vnderstand the nature of the word diuorce, *à diuertendo*—
>
> MOR. No excursions vpon words, good Doctor, to the question briefly.
>
> CVT. I answere then, the Canon-law affords diuorce but in few cases, and the principall is in the common case, the adulterous case. But there are *duodecim impedimenta*, twelue impediments (as we call 'hem) all which doe not *dirimere contractum*, but *irritum reddere matrimonium*, as wee say in the Canon-law, *not take away the bond, but cause a nullitie therein*.
>
> MOR. I vnderstood you, before: good sir, auoid your impertinencie of translation.[20]

With their stock of Latin terms, their needless digressions, and their disputations between themselves, Cutbeard and Otter are thoroughly convincing to Morose. His critical attitude toward the professional jargon of lawyers, with which the audience must sympathize, is therefore partly responsible for his being gulled and tormented. Truewit, in speaking apparently for Jonson, the traditional satirist, had hoped that the disguises would be made "without wronging the dignitie of either profession, since they are but persons put on, and for mirths sake, to torment him." [21] The value of the jargon in this scene is dramatic rather than merely satiric. But the scene would not be so effective as drama if it were not so pointed as satire. In *Epicoene* jargon has become more intimately related to the dramatic action as a whole than in any previous play of Jonson's. The lan-

[20] *Ibid.*, V, iii, 70–83 (V, 258–59).   [21] *Ibid.*, IV, vii, 48–50 (V, 250).

guage of Sir John Daw has a wider significance than that of, say, Fastidious Brisk, because it has a greater bearing on a dramatic action. Jargon has become a means by which characters interact upon one another.

The Alchemist (1610) represents the crowning point in the history of Jonson's use of jargon. No other play is so thoroughly permeated by it. The jargons of the alchemists and the Puritans, especially, are of central dramatic importance.

The language of alchemists was traditionally regarded as a jargon, and had been so used in English literature even as early as Chaucer.[22] In the *Discoverie of Witchcraft* (1584), Reginald Scot acknowledges a debt to Chaucer in his treatment of alchemy. He also explains that "because the practisers heere of would be thought wise, they have devised words of art, sentences and epithets obscure. . . . For what plaine man would not beleeve, that they are learned and jollie fellowes, that have in such readinesse so many mysticall termes of art."[23] Their language, used as jargon, had even been turned to account in early Elizabethan drama. The subplot of Lyly's *Gallathea* is the story of Rafe's fortune-seeking, and especially his employment by an alchemist. But although the rhetorical quality of the language of the alchemists had been recognized in English literature before Jonson, neither Chaucer nor Lyly uses the actual terms of alchemy with such dramatic effectiveness. In Chaucer's tale, the terms are used rather in the description of the Canon's craft than in the tale of cozening which the Canon's Yeoman tells. That is, they have little or no part in the dialogue between the canon and the priest of the tale. The Canon's use of the jargon is described at the beginning of the Yeoman's tale:

> In al this world of falshede nis his peer;
> For in his termes he wol hym so wynde,

[22] His Canon's Yeoman says, "we semen wonder wise, Oure termes been so clergial and so queynte" (*Canterbury Tales*, G 751-52, in *Works*, ed. F. N. Robinson, Boston, 1933, p. 258).

[23] Reginald Scot, *The Discoverie of Witchcraft*, ed. Brinsley Nicholson (London, 1886), p. 294.

And speke his wordes in so sly a kynde,
Whanne he commune shal with any wight,
That he wol make hym doten anonright,
But it a feend be, as hymselen is.[24]

The action of the tale turns, however, not on the use of "termes"
by the canon, but on his sleight of hand.

In *Gallathea* also, the jargon of alchemy is used principally
in description; Peter, "the Alcumist's boy," soliloquizes:

What a life doe I leade with my Maister, nothing but blowing of
bellows, beating of spirits, & scraping of Croslets? it is a very se-
crete Science, for none almost can vnderstand the language of it.
Sublimation, Almigation, Calcination, Rubification, Encorpora-
tion, Circination, Sementation, Albification, and Frementation.
With as many termes vnpossible to be vttered, as the Arte to be
compassed.[25]

Peter is a naïve character, and has some claim on the sympathy
of the audience. The language which he uses does not make
him either a comic butt or a knave. The spectator enjoys his
sense of humor. His language resembles that of Jonson's *Mercury Vindicated* rather than that of *The Alchemist.* In the
masque, Mercury escapes from a furnace in an alchemist's work-
shop, and describes his torture by "old Smug of Lemnos, and his
smoky family." The terms are used in satiric description; Vul-
can calls Mercury a "scorner," which is his name for a critic,
but the tone of Mercury's speech is light. Like Peter in *Gallathea,* he has a sense of humor, and makes a claim upon our sympathy:

I am their Crude, and their Sublimate; their Præcipitate, and their
vnctuous; their male and their female; sometimes their *Her-
maphrodite;* what they list to stile me. It is I, that am corroded,
and exalted, and sublim'd, and reduc'd, and fetch'd ouer, and
filtred, and wash'd, and wip'd; what betweene their salts and their
sulphures; their oyles and their tartars, their brines and their vine-

[24] *Canterbury Tales,* G 979–84, in *Works,* ed. Robinson, p. 260.
[25] *Gallathea,* II, iii, 9–15, in Lyly's *Works,* ed. R. W. Bond (3 vols., Oxford, 1902), II, 442.

gers, you might take me out now a sous'd *Mercury*, now a salted *Mercury*, now a smok'd and dri'd *Mercury*, now a pouldred and pickl'd *Mercury*: neuer Herring, Oyster, or Coucumer past so many vexations. . . .[26]

Description of this kind, in both Lyly's play and Jonson's masque, lacks the immediacy of drama. In actual dialogue, Lyly makes a limited use of the terms when Peter tries to interest Rafe in his master's work, so that he can escape:

> RAFFE. Howe might a man serue him and learne hys cunning?
> PETER. Easilie. First seeme to vnderstand the termes, and speciallie marke these points. In our Arte there are foure Spirits.[27]

He then names the spirits, and is about to name the "seauen bodies" when the alchemist himself appears. The master's conversation with Rafe is taken up with the conventional questions. On his first appearance he must explain why, "beeing so cunning," he "should be so ragged," while, in a later scene, he finds the usual excuses for his want of success ("if there be a cole too much, or a sparke too little, if it be a little too hote, or a thought too softe, all our labour is in vaine").[28] But the jargon has little influence on the action.

In a scene of *Eastward Ho* (1605), which seems surely to have been contributed by Jonson, the jargon of alchemy is used, not in description but in dramatic dialogue. Quicksilver uses the terms deliberately in order to win the admiration and confidence of Petronel and Seagull. He makes no attempt, however, to gull his victims; he says frankly to them that "the tearmes of this Arte, euery ignorant Quack-saluer is perfect in," [29] and, after winning their approval, hopes that "this is enough to put some spirit into the liuers of you." [30]

The remarkable dramatic exposition of the opening scene of *The Alchemist* has frequently been observed. A special lan-

---

[26] *Mercury Vindicated from the Alchemists*, ll. 51–61 (VII, 410–11).
[27] *Gallathea*, II, iii, 47–49 (ed. Bond, II, 443).
[28] *Ibid.*, III, iii, 15–16 (ed. Bond, II, 451).
[29] *Eastward Ho*, IV, i, 219–20 (IV, 583).   [30] *Ibid.*, IV, i, 237–38 (IV, 584).

guage which is so important in the action of the play as a whole is used quite naturally in this scene between the two knaves, as a source of personal invective. In demanding more respect, Face recalls Subtle's past for him:

> When all your *alchemy*, and your *algebra*,
> Your *mineralls*, *vegetalls*, and *animalls*,
> Your coniuring, cosning, and your dosen of trades,
> Could not relieue your corps, with so much linnen
> Would make you tinder, but to see a fire.[31]

The sarcasm of Face's use of the terms is sharpened by alliteration and rhyme. Temporarily on the side of intelligence, he helps to establish a critical attitude in the audience. In Subtle's counterblast, he also uses the terms of alchemy:

> Thou vermine, haue I tane thee, out of dung,
> So poore, so wretched, when no liuing thing
> Would keepe thee companie, but a spider, or worse?
> Rais'd thee from broomes, and dust, and watring pots?
> *Sublim'd* thee, and *exalted* thee, and *fix'd* thee
> I' the *third region*, call'd our *state of grace?*
> Wrought thee to *spirit*, to *quintessence*, with paines
> Would twise haue won me the *philosophers worke?* [32]

Face understands Subtle's game, and the audience recognizes at once the rhetorical use of alchemical terms. Subtle himself later mentions the speech as rhetorical: "I onely vs'd those speeches, as a spurre To him." [33] After witnessing this half-playful altercation, the audience is prepared to watch, and even to anticipate with interest, Subtle's rhetoric at work. The opening scene thus introduces not only the situation but also the special language in which much of the play is written, and establishes an attitude toward it. The need is partly eliminated for comments in the dialogue to guide the reactions of the audience to the language of certain characters.

Subtle and Face join in using the jargon of alchemy to gull

[31] *The Alchemist*, I, i, 38–42 (V, 296).   [32] *Ibid.*, I, i, 64–71 (V, 297).
[33] *Ibid.*, I, i, 158–59 (V, 300).

Sir Epicure Mammon, and he adopts their language as his own.
Amazed at Surly's skepticism, he asks him:

> Doe you thinke, I fable with you? I assure you,
> He that has once the *flower of the sunne*,
> The perfect *ruby*, which we call *elixir*,
> Not onely can doe that, . . .[34]

He refers to himself and the alchemists as "we," and is thoroughly confident that he understands the meaning of their
terms. The rhetorical quality escapes him. The contrast between his naïve use of the language, and Face's mastery of it,
appears in a later scene, when Face amplifies an argument by
using the alchemist's names for the changing colors of his con-
coction:

> . . . These bleard-eyes
> Haue wak'd, to read your seuerall colours, sir,
> Of the *pale citron*, the *greene lyon*, the *crow*,
> The *peacocks taile*, the *plumed swan*.
>
> MAM.   And, lastly,
> Thou hast descryed the *flower*, the *sanguis agni?*
> FAC.   Yes, sir.[35]

Mammon's superficial familiarity with the jargon persuades him
that he understands alchemy, and his own use of the terms com-
pletes the gulling which Face began. Jonson thus concentrates
forceful irony in the simple phrase, "Yes, sir." Mammon does
not need to be persuaded any more. He can only think of life
after projection:

> . . . I will make me, a back
> With the *elixir*, that shall be as tough
> As HERCVLES, to encounter fiftie a night.
> Th'art sure, thou saw'st it *bloud?*[36]

The question interposed is clearly from the surface of his mind,
a deliberate concession to Surly's skepticism. His use of the
technical term indicates his own implicit confidence in the final

[34] *Ibid.*, II, i, 46–49 (V, 315).   [35] *Ibid.*, II, ii, 24–29 (V, 318).
[36] *Ibid.*, II, ii, 37–40 (V, 319).

outcome. He continues to picture his soft beds and perfumed rooms:

> . . . and my baths, like pits
> To fall into: from whence, we will come forth,
> And rowle vs drie in gossamour, and roses.
> (Is it arriu'd at *ruby?*)—[37]

The question here, no less superficial than the first, is perhaps meant to be suggested to him by the association of *"ruby"* with the image of "roses" in his mind. Surly calls attention to what Mammon does in the play:

> Hart! can it be,
> That a graue sir, a rich, that has no need,
> A wise sir, too, at other times, should thus
> With his owne oathes, and arguments, make hard meanes
> To gull himselfe? [38]

Because Mammon accepts it so willingly, Subtle's rhetoric for him need contain nothing but the affectedly obscure vocabulary which alchemists were commonly known to use.[39] But Surly is critical: "What a braue language here is? next to canting."

In dealing with Surly's criticism, Subtle has to adapt his language to "a new tune," and the rhetorical skill with which he does so must have impressed a Jacobean audience. He undertakes, for Surly's instruction, to describe the change from "remote matter" into gold. Of the former he says:

> It is, of the one part,
> A humide exhalation, which we call
> *Materia liquida*, or the *vnctuous water;*
> On th'other part, a certaine crasse, and viscous

---

[37] *Ibid.*, II, ii, 50–53 (V, 319).   [38] *Ibid.*, II, iii, 278–82 (V, 330).
[39] "We sometimes employ words new and unheard of, not (as Alchemists are wont to do) in order to veil things with a pedantic terminology and to make them dark and obscure, but in order that hidden things which have no name . . . may be plainly and fully published" (William Gilbert, *De Magnete*, 1600, tr. P. F. Mottelay, New York, 1893, p. 1).

Portion of earth; both which, concorporate,
Doe make the elementarie matter of gold:
Which is not, yet, *propria materia*,
But commune to all mettalls, and all stones.
For, where it is forsaken of that moysture,
And hath more drynesse, it becomes a stone;
Where it retaines more of the humid fatnesse,
It turnes to *sulphur*, or to *quick-siluer:*
Who are the parents of all other mettalls.
Nor can this remote matter, sodainly,
Progresse so from extreme, vnto extreme,
As to grow gold, and leape ore all the meanes.
Nature doth, first, beget th'imperfect; then
Proceedes shee to the perfect. Of that ayrie,
And oily water, *mercury* is engendred;
Sulphure o' the fat, and earthy part: the one
(Which is the last) supplying the place of male,
The other of the female, in all mettalls.
Some doe beleeue *hermaphrodeitie*,
That both doe act, and suffer. But, . . .[40]

The dispassionate tone of this speech depends partly upon its leisurely progress and length. Subtle cuts his technical vocabulary down to what he implies is an irreducible minimum, offering descriptive definitions and alternative terms in the pretended attempt to be clear. The terms are introduced apologetically (". . . which we call . . ."), and the tone is that of exposition, not argument. A spirit of reason pervades the entire speech ("Nor can this . . . Progresse so . . ."), and dogmatism is avoided ("Some doe beleeue"). Surly is not persuaded, however, even by this studied rhetoric, which is so much more elaborate than Mammon required. "I'll beleeue," he says,

That *Alchemie* is a pretty kind of game,
Somewhat like tricks o' the cards, to cheat a man,
With charming.
Svb.   Sir?
Svr.   What else are all your termes,
Whereon no one o' your writers grees with other?

[40] *The Alchemist,* II, iii, 142–65 (V, 326).

Of your *elixir*, your *lac virginis*,
Your *stone*, your *med'cine*, and your *chrysosperme*,
Your *sal*, your *sulphur*, and your *mercurie*,
Your *oyle of height*, your *tree of life*, your *bloud*,
Your *marchesite*, your *tutie*, your *magnesia*,
Your *toade*, your *crow*, your *dragon*, and your *panthar*,
Your *sunne*, your *moone*, your *firmament*, your *adrop*,
Your *lato*, *azoch*, *zernich*, *chibrit*, *heautarit*,
And then, your *red man*, and your *white woman*,
With all your broths, your *menstrues*, and *materialls*,
Of pisse, and egge-shells, womens termes, mans bloud,
Haire o' the head, burnt clouts, chalke, merds, and clay,
Poulder of bones, scalings of iron, glasse,
And worlds of other strange *ingredients*,
Would burst a man to name? [41]

Surly's attitude is sensible, and the audience feels it natural to agree with his argument. Yet Subtle's speech is certainly more reasonable and convincing. It is less obviously rhetorical, and does not simply beg the question like Surly's. When Surly is silenced, the audience is persuaded not that he is wrong, but that Subtle's rhetorical power is great enough to carry the weight it does in the play. Subtle does not reject the general implication that the terms are fundamentally meaningless, and he is supported by Mammon with strong effect:

> And all these, nam'd
> Intending but one thing: which art our writers
> Vs'd to obscure their art.
> MAM.   Sir, so I told him,
> Because the simple idiot should not learne it,
> And make it vulgar.[42]

Jargon does not have the effect of seeming to obscure the art from Mammon. On the contrary, as soon as he becomes superficially familiar with the language of the alchemists, he convinces himself that he understands their art. Like many of Jonson's dupes, he confuses words with knowledge.

One of the sources of Jonson's remarkable power in the dra-

[41] *Ibid.*, II, iii, 179–98 (V, 327).   [42] *Ibid.*, II, iii, 198–202 (V, 327).

matic use of affected speech is his capacity for varying it. Subtle prepares for a third variation of the alchemist's jargon when Ananias appears:

> Now,
> In a new tune, new gesture, but old language.[43]

The new tune is suggested at once in the rhythm of his speech:

SVB.	Where is my drudge?
FAC.	Sir.

SVB.   Take away the *recipient*,
And rectifie your *menstrue*, from the *phlegma*.
Then powre it, o' the *Sol*, in the *cucurbite*,
And let 'hem macerate, together.

FAC.   Yes, sir.
And saue the ground?

SVB.   No. *Terra damnata*
Must not haue entrance, in the *worke*.[44]

The dogmatic tone, which is in marked contrast to Subtle's address to Surly, is apparently calculated to impress the "*faithfull Brother*." "*Terra damnata*," which in alchemy means simply condemned refuse, is used by Subtle at this point to suggest to ignorant Ananias the religious purity of the "*worke*." In addition to technical words, Subtle weights his speech with Latinisms like "rectifie" and "macerate," part of the jargon which all learned professions, and all others who affected learning, had in common. After giving Face his orders in such a way as to impress Ananias, he turns to the latter and asks brusquely: "Who are you?" Ananias replies, confident of his own speech: "A *faithfull Brother*, if it please you." The audience is at once introduced to a rich comic theme, the pitting of one professional jargon against another. In so far as they are pure jargon, they are like two different languages, and misunderstanding is not unnatural. Subtle is a master of words, however, and his misunderstanding is only pretense:

---

[43] *Ibid.*, II, iv, 26–27 (V, 333).   [44] *Ibid.*, II, v, 1–6 (V, 334).

> What's that?
> A *Lullianist?* a *Ripley? Filius artis?*
> Can you *sublime,* and *dulcefie? calcine?*
> Know you the *sapor pontick? sapor stiptick?*
> Or, what is *homogene,* or *heterogene?* [45]

As if he takes him for one of his own brotherhood, Subtle questions him on his discipleship, and on his knowledge of the processes, products, and qualities of things used by the alchemists. The whole is calculated to bully Ananias into complete submission, but unlike Mammon he has a faith and a language of his own which give him the confidence to despise anyone else's: "I vnderstand no *heathen* language, truely." Again Subtle pretends to understand "*heathen,*" not in Ananias's special sense, but as any terminology foreign to alchemy. He names more terms in an attempt to subdue Ananias, but a naïve firmness makes the brother only comment:

> Heathen Greeke, I take it.
> SVB. How? *heathen Greeke?*
> ANA.   All's *heathen,* but the *Hebrew.*[46]

Subtle seems nearly stopped at this point. Instead of being at once effective, his jargon is rebuffed by the cant phrases with which Ananias is armed. He calls on Face for an additional barrage of words:

> SVB.   Sirah, my varlet, stand you forth, and speake to him,
>   Like a *Philosopher:* Answere, i'the language.
>   Name the vexations, and the martyrizations
>   Of mettals, in the worke.
> FAC.   Sir, *Putrefaction,*
>   *Solution, Ablution, Sublimation,*
>   *Cohobation, Calcination, Ceration,* and
>   *Fixation.*
> SVB.   This is *heathen Greeke,* to you, now?
>   And when comes *Viuification?*
> FAC.   After *Mortification.*

[45] *Ibid.,* II, v, 7-11 (V, 334).   [46] *Ibid.,* II, v, 16-17 (V, 334).

SVB.   What's *Cohobation?*
FAC.   'Tis the powring on
        Your *Aqua Regis*, and then drawing him off,
        To the *trine circle* of the *seuen spheares*.[47]

Subtle's "new tune" here is to present "the language" in a cate-
chism; his final question is the definition of "your *lapis philo-
sophicus*," to which Face replies:

                    'Tis a *stone*, and not
        A *stone;* a *spirit*, a *soule*, and a *body:*
        Which, if you doe dissolue, it is dissolu'd,
        If you *coagulate*, it is *coagulated*,
        If you make it to *flye*, it *flyeth*.[48]

This is clearly an adaptation of the speech of the "*holy Consis-
torie*" itself, which Subtle and Face seem to believe is the only
language which Ananias understands or can be moved by. After
this performance by Face, Subtle says "enough," but Ananias is
not subdued yet:

        The *Brethren* bid me say vnto you, sir.
        Surely, they will not venter any more,
        Till they may see *proiection*.[49]

Subtle is incapable of dealing with him, and asks his name, which
he uses as a pretext for sending him away:

                            Out, the varlet
        That cossend the *Apostles!* Hence, away,
        Flee *Mischiefe;* had your *holy Consistorie*
        No name to send me, of another sound;
        Then wicked ANANIAS? Send your *Elders*,
        Hither, to make atonement for you, quickly.
        And gi' me satisfaction; or out-goes
        The fire: and downe th'*alembekes*, and the fornace,
        Piger Henricus, or what not. Thou wretch,
        Both *Sericon*, and *Bufo*, shall be lost,
        Tell 'hem. All hope of rooting out the *Bishops*,
        Or th'*Antichristian Hierarchie* shall perish,

47 *Ibid.*, II, v, 18–28 (V, 334–35).   48 *Ibid.*, II, v, 40–44 (V, 335).
49 *Ibid.*, II, v, 64–66 (V, 336).

If they stay threescore minutes. The *Aqueitie,*
Terreitie, and *Sulphureitie*
Shall runne together againe, and all be annull'd,
Thou wicked ANANIAS.[50]

There is a calculated balance here between the jargon of alchemy and that of the Puritans. "Atonement," "*Bishops,*"
"*Antichristian Hierarchie,*" "wicked" have a special weight for
Ananias, while the technical terms of alchemy are intended to
frighten him by the mysterious threat which they seem to conceal. It is the word, nothing more, that matters; it is not simply
that "Both *Sericon,* and *Bufo,* shall be lost," but that Ananias
must "tell 'hem" so.

When Ananias returns with his teacher Tribulation, Subtle
uses terms [51] which enlarge upon the destruction that was
threatened if they had not returned in "threescore minutes."
The terms have a greater weight with the more worldly Tribulation than they had with Ananias, who only "hath a com-
petent knowledge" of the truth, Tribulation says, "by reuela-
tion." [52] Subtle speaks mysteriously when Tribulation asks him
how long the "*Saints*" must wait:

                                        Let me see,
How's the moone, now? Eight, nine, ten dayes hence
He will be *siluer potate;* then, three dayes,
Before he *citronise:* some fifteene dayes,
The *Magisterium* will be perfected.[53]

Ananias interrupts the calculations with a leading question like
Mammon's:

        About the second day, of the third weeke
        In the ninth month?
SVB.   Yes, my good ANANIAS.[54]

Thus he gulls himself, but unlike Mammon he has not adopted
Subtle's language. He is gulled by his own jargon, which seems

[50] *Ibid.,* II, v, 72–87 (V, 336–37).   [51] *Ibid.,* III, ii, 1–6 (V, 342).
[52] *Ibid.,* III, ii, 113–14 (V, 346).   [53] *Ibid.,* III, ii, 126–30 (V, 346).
[54] *Ibid.,* III, ii, 131–32 (V, 346).

to have been brought into play here by the suggestion in his mind of Subtle's words, "eight, nine, ten dayes hence . . . then three dayes."

Later in the play, the jargon of alchemy is used incidentally; a sustained use is rare. When Mammon's hopes are to be disposed of, there is "*A great crack and noise within,*" which Face reports:

> O sir, we are defeated! all the *workes*
> Are flowne *in fumo:* euery glasse is burst.
> Fornace, and all rent downe! as if a bolt
> Of thunder had beene driuen through the house.
> *Retorts, Receiuers, Pellicanes, Bolt-heads,*
> All strooke in shiuers! [55]

The description, for Mammon's ear, is the final link in the ingenious plot against him, but it lacks the dramatic intensity of the jargon in the first three acts. At a Harvard performance of *The Alchemist,*[56] the first acts seemed to hold more interest for the audience than the solution at the end. Such an unusual effect is a comment on the interest which is aroused even in a modern audience by Jonson's dramatic use of rhetoric.

It has already been observed how Subtle was forced to adopt some Puritan terms in order to break down the stiff resistance of Ananias. He uses Puritan phrases also when he meets Mammon, for, as an alchemist, he had a reputation for piety. Surly says:

> Why, I haue heard, he must be *homo frugi,*
> A pious, holy, and religious man,
> One free from mortall sinne, a very virgin.[57]

Subtle maintains this reputation by using the proper words. He warns Mammon, at their first meeting, against a "carnall appetite" and "vngouern'd haste," phrases which acquired a special

[55] *Ibid.,* IV, v, 57–62 (V, 378).
[56] Eliot House, Harvard University, December 19, 1939.
[57] *The Alchemist,* II, ii, 97–99 (V, 320).

solemnity by their use among Puritans. The irony of this speech depends upon the use of such cant phrases. Subtle's fears are justified when he says, "I doubt yo'are couetous." The Puritan language forms an important element in the plot by which Mammon is made to gull himself, and blame only himself ("O, my voluptuous mind"). Subtle uses Puritan jargon in order to maintain appearances which the audience easily sees through, but he expresses at the same time some real truths about Mammon. The folly of Epicure Mammon makes him see only the appearance, and be blind both to Subtle's disguise and, because of that disguise, to the truth which he expresses. The plot is Subtle's own, and he is therefore able here at the beginning to prophesy the end:

> If you, my sonne, should now preuaricate,
> And, to your owne particular lusts, employ
> So great, and catholique a blisse: be sure,
> A curse will follow, yea, and ouertake
> Your subtle, and most secret wayes.[58]

Later, when Subtle makes the planned discovery of Mammon with Doll Common, he speaks the same language, and with similar irony uses the common rhetorical device of accusing Mammon of artifice in the choice of words:

SVB.　　　　　　　　　How! What sight is here!
Close deeds of darknesse, and that shunne the light!
Bring him againe. Who is he? What, my sonne!
O, I haue liu'd too long.

MAM.　　　　　　　　　Nay good, deare father,
There was no'vnchast purpose.

SVB.　　　　　　　　　Not? and flee me,
When I come in?

MAM.　　　　　　　That was my error.

SVB.　　　　　　　　　　Error?
Guilt, guilt, my sonne, giue it the right name. No maruaile,
If I found check in our *great worke* within,
When such affaires as these were managing! [59]

---

[58] *Ibid.*, II, iii, 19-23 (V, 321).　　　　[59] *Ibid.*, IV, v, 33-41 (V, 377).

Subtle's use of Puritan jargon is quite different when he addresses Ananias and Tribulation, to whom it is familiar. In his
long speech to Tribulation enumerating some of the possible
uses of the "*Stone*," he reaches the general conclusion that "you
may be any thing"; then follows a further enumeration of common actions which the "*Brethren*" may now "leaue off." No
longer need they

> make zealous wiues
> To rob their husbands, for the *common cause:*
> Nor take the start of bonds, broke but one day,
> And say, *they were forfeited, by prouidence.*
> Nor shall you need, ore-night to eate huge meales,
> To celebrate your next daies fast the better:
> The whilst the *Brethren*, and the *Sisters*, humbled,
> Abate the stiffenesse of the flesh. Nor cast
> Before your hungrie hearers, scrupulous bones,
> As whether a *Christian* may hawke, or hunt;
> Or whether, *Matrons, of the holy assembly*,
> May lay their haire out, or weare doublets:
> Or haue that idoll *Starch*, about their linnen.[60]

The language has one meaning for the audience, but quite another for Ananias and Tribulation. The fact that neither appreciates the sarcasm, and that both are persuaded by the whole
speech, emphasizes how uncritically they use and accept these
cant phrases, which put a stamp of approval on any argument.
When Subtle sarcastically speaks of "that idoll *Starch*" in the
midst of a lengthy argument, Ananias interposes, "It is, indeed,
an idoll," and the more sophisticated Tribulation, who seems to
follow the argument, but not to appreciate its ridicule, says,
"Pray you, sir, goe on." Subtle points out that they will no
longer have to adopt personal names

> Onely for glorie, and to catch the eare
> Of the *Disciple*

and Tribulation, without disagreeing, adds:

> they are
> Wayes, that the *godly Brethren* haue inuented,

[60] *Ibid.*, III, ii, 70–82 (V, 344–45).

> For propagation of the *glorious cause*,
> As very notable meanes, and whereby, also,
> Themselues grow soone, and profitably famous.[61]

The two brethren are not taken in by a jargon unfamiliar to
them, nor by their own jargon used simply as persuasive speech
by a clever speaker. Subtle's language seems sarcastic to the
audience. In this scene the Puritans gull themselves just as
surely as Mammon did earlier in the play. A simpler exploita-
tion of the special value attached to certain words by Ananias
is illustrated later in the play. When Surly has nearly succeeded
in exposing Subtle and all his work, and the quarreling
dimensions of Kastril are already loosed upon him, Ananias
demands:

> | | What is the motiue? |
> | --- | --- |
> | Svb. | Zeale, in the yong gentleman, |
> | | Against his *Spanish* slops— |
> | Ana. | They are profane, |
> | | Leud, superstitious, and idolatrous breeches.[62] |

The single word "Zeale," which Subtle uses knowingly, suc-
ceeds in drawing forth Ananias's stock of epithets regardless of
their ineptitude.

In the scene between Ananias and Tribulation at the beginning of Act III, their jargon is first used as a part of decorum,
and identifies the characters:

> | Tri. | These chastisements are common to the *Saints*, |
> | --- | --- |
> | | And such rebukes we of the *Separation* |
> | | Must beare, with willing shoulders, as the trialls |
> | | Sent forth, to tempt our frailties. |
> | Ana. | In pure zeale, |
> | | I doe not like the man: He is a *heathen*. |
> | | And speakes the language of *Canaan*, truely.[63] |

But in this scene the jargon has another important dramatic
function, because it makes it possible to justify for the over-

---

[61] *Ibid.*, III, ii, 96–101 (V, 345). [62] *Ibid.*, IV, vii, 47–49 (V, 384).
[63] *Ibid.*, III, i, 1–6 (V, 340–41).

zealous Ananias the dealings of the *"Saints"* with what Tribulation confesses is a "prophane person, indeed."

TRI.	Good *Brother*, we must bend vnto all meanes,
	That may giue furtherance, to the *holy cause.*
ANA.	Which his cannot: The *sanctified cause*
	Should haue a *sanctified course.*

TRI.   Not alwaies necessary.
The children of perdition are, oft-times,
Made instruments euen of the greatest workes.
Beside, we should giue somewhat to mans nature,
The place he liues in, still about the fire,
And fume of mettalls, that intoxicate
The braine of man, and make him prone to passion.
Where haue you greater *Atheists*, then your Cookes?
Or more prophane, or cholerick then your Glasse-men?
More *Antichristian*, then your Bell-founders?
What makes the Deuill so deuillish, I would aske you,
Sathan, our common enemie, but his being
Perpetually about the fire, and boyling
Brimstone, and *arsnike?* We must giue, I say,
Vnto the motiues, and the stirrers vp
Of humours in the bloud. It may be so,
When as the *worke* is done, the *stone* is made,
This heate of his may turne into a zeale,
And stand vp for the *beauteous discipline*,
Against the menstruous cloth, and ragg of *Rome*.
We must await his calling, and the comming
Of the good spirit. You did fault, t'vpbraid him
With the *Brethrens* blessing of *Heidelberg*, waighing
What need we haue, to hasten on the worke,
For the restoring of the *silenc'd Saints*,
Which ne'er will be, but by the *Philosophers stone*.
And, so a learned *Elder*, one of *Scotland*,
Assur'd me; *Aurum potabile* being
The onely med'cine, for the ciuill *Magistrate*,
T'incline him to a feeling of the cause:
And must be daily vs'd, in the disease.[64]

Throughout this speech, cant words are used to make the de-
praved arguments more acceptable to Ananias. The coloration-

[64] *Ibid.*, III, i, 11–44 (V, 341–42).

value of "the *holy cause*" at the beginning should have been
sufficient to conclude the argument were it not for his inspired
stubbornness. In answer to Ananias's objection, Tribulation
argues that since Subtle is unfortunately subject to the same hot
vapors which make atheists, antichristians, and Satan himself
(all bogey words for Ananias) he who "may" some day stand
up for the *"beauteous discipline"* surely should be tolerated.
This is in answer to Ananias's first objection. Tribulation then
proceeds to the more practical and more real argument, but in
order not to offend the religious scruples of Ananias he carefully defines it only in acceptable words. That they have the
right effect is shown by Ananias's exclamation:

> I haue not edified more, truely, by man;
> Not, since the *beautifull light*, first, shone on me.[65]

Ananias is shown in this scene to use the Puritan jargon on a
different plane from his master Tribulation. He is victimized by
the jargon; Tribulation has mastered it. There is something of
the knave-gull relationship between the two. The quality of
Ananias's speech is brought out again in the later scene in which
he and Kastril cry down Surly. A parallel is suggested between
Ananias's unthinking use of a limited stock of words, and Kastril's ignorantly affected oaths and curses.

Subtle and Face adopt a special jargon in gulling Kastril.
When Face learns from Drugger that "a gentleman, newly
warme in'his land" has come up to learn "to carry quarrells, As
gallants doe," he says:

> 'Slid, NAB! The Doctor is the onely man
> In *Christendome* for him. He has made a table,
> With *Mathematicall* demonstrations,
> Touching the Art of quarrells. He will giue him
> An instrument to quarrell by.[66]

Face uses technical language in describing the Doctor's instru-
ment to Kastril:

[65] *Ibid.*, III, i, 45–46 (V, 342).   [66] *Ibid.*, II, vi, 65–69 (V, 339).

> . . . no sooner shall you make report
> Of any quarrell, but he will take the height on't,
> Most instantly; and tell in what degree,
> Of saf'ty it lies in, or mortalitie.
> And, how it may be borne, whether in a *right line*,
> Or a *halfe-circle;* or may, else, be cast
> Into an *angle blunt*, if not *acute:*
> All this he will demonstrate. And then, rules,
> To giue, and take the lie, by.

KAS.   How? to take it?

FAC.   Yes, in *oblique*, hee'll shew you; or in *circle:*
> But neuer in *diameter*. The whole towne
> Studie his *theoremes*, and dispute them, ordinarily,
> At the eating *Academies.*[67]

The geometric terms are a parody upon the technical language of the Italian school of fencing, in which the art was an applied geometry. Face's use of the terms is rhetorically effective, but when he descends to plain English and speaks of rules to take the lie by, Kastril questions him, and makes him scurry back into the safe obscurity of special terms. Jonson frequently makes his knaves speak ambiguously, as if to protect themselves against a charge of lying. When the audience sees a meaning which certain characters fail to see, a new element of irony is introduced. In the last sentence Face means either that it is customary in the "*Academies*" for men to argue for and against the Doctor's theories, or that it is customary for the whole town to question them. Kastril apparently understands only the first meaning.

Face or Subtle may be expected to introduce any kind of language that will serve their purposes of deception. In presenting Dapper, the lawyer's clerk, Face finds an appropriate use of a law term. He pretends to be annoyed with Subtle's lack of interest in Dapper's fee:

FAC.   I am sorry,
> I e're imbarqu'd my selfe, in such a businesse.

[67] *Ibid.*, III, iv, 29–41 (V, 351–52). When Subtle as professor of quarrels meets Kastril, he uses a different stock of terms (IV, ii, 16–33).

DAP.   Nay, good sir. He did call you.

FAC.   Will he take, then?

SVB.   First, heare me—

FAC.   Not a syllable, 'lesse you take.

SVB.   Pray ye', sir—

FAC.   Vpon no termes, but an *assumpsit*.

SVB.   Your humor must be law.

FAC.   Why now, sir, talke.
          Now, I dare heare you with mine honour. Speake.[68]

Both Face and Subtle speak ambiguously, but only one meaning
is conveyed to Dapper. To him Face seems to say that he will
listen to Subtle only according to the terms of an unwritten
contract which they may agree upon. "Termes" to Subtle is
much more likely to suggest law terms like "*assumpsit*" in
which, Face seems to say, his suit should be worded so as to
impress Dapper. When Subtle replies, "Your humor must be
law," he means (1) that Face's stubbornly maintained demand
must rule, or (2) that he sees that under the circumstances Face
is bound to employ legal terms, or possibly, (3) that it must be
Face's "humor," not his own, to use the legal terms which Face
suggests. Such ambiguities are not uncommon in the speech of
Jonson's knaves. Ambiguous terms are to be used, according to
Aristotle, when the intention is deliberately to mislead. "Long
circumlocution takes in the hearers, who find themselves affected like the majority of those who listen to the soothsay-
ers." [69] Jonson's knaves use technical jargon with the rhetorical
purpose to which Aristotle here refers.

Jonson may well have been aware of the maturity of his
achievement in *The Alchemist*. In the year after it was produced
he wrote his second tragedy, *Catiline* (1611), and in 1612 he
began to prepare his famous *Works*, published in folio in 1616.
The language of *Catiline* is highly rhetorical, but it is not
marked by the presence of jargon. With the exception of a
few terms affected by the women politicians, jargon seems

---

[68] *Ibid.*, I, ii, 65–71 (V, 304–5).
[69] *Rhetoric*, III, v (Loeb Classical Library, p. 373).

to have been excluded from the play as unbefitting a tragedy.

After completing the job of editing his works for the first Folio, Jonson turned with characteristic vigor to new experiment in *Bartholomew Fair* (1614). Its language, however, like that of other Jonsonian comedies is marked by jargon. As in *The Alchemist*, the Puritan characters use jargon as rhetoric to disguise their hypocrisy. Tribulation religiously justifies his desire for gold; Zeal Busy, his gluttonous appetite. As in *The Alchemist* also, Jonson prepares the audience to listen critically to the rhetoric before it is actually used in the dialogue. Before they appear the speech of Zeal Busy and Purecraft is described and illustrated by Purecraft's daughter, Win-the-Fight, and her husband, John Littlewit. John wishes to visit the Fair, but his wife doubts whether her Puritanical mother would ever consent to such a *"prophane motion."* He conceives a plot whereby his wife will long, regretfully and in Puritan terms, to eat pig "i' the heart o'the *Fayre.*" Win is confident that she "can be *Hypocrite* enough," and the audience is introduced to a dramatic situation in which language is adapted to the aim of deception. Even though the Littlewits understand the value of translating the question for Purecraft into religious terms, Purecraft's reaction is automatic and unbending. She is tempted by the prospect of a visit to the Fair, but, like Ananias, she is condemned to be consistent until she can find religious authority for being otherwise. "What shall we doe? call our zealous brother *Busy* hither, for his faithfull fortification in this charge of the aduersary; child, my deare childe, you shall eate Pigge, be comforted, my sweet child." [70] She seems to say that Zeal Busy will help to fortify them against temptation; what her words may mean, however, is that Zeal Busy will fortify them to meet and accept "this charge of the aduersary." She is depending upon his rhetorical and dialectical skill to justify, on purely religious grounds, the eating of pig in the Fair. Purecraft addresses Zeal Busy confident that he will find a way:

[70] *Bartholomew Fair*, I, vi, 25–28 (VI, 37).

O brother *Busy!* your helpe heere to edifie, and raise vs vp in a scruple; my daughter *Win-the-fight* is visited with a naturall disease of women; call'd, A longing to eate Pigge.

Ioн[N]. I Sir, a *Bartholmew*-pigge: and in the *Fayre.*

Pvr[craft]. And I would be satisfied from you, Religiouslywise, whether a widdow of the sanctified assembly, or a widdowes daughter, may commit the act, without offence to the weaker sisters.

Bvs[y]. Verily, for the disease of longing, it is a disease, a carnall disease, or appetite, incident to women: and as it is carnall, and incident, it is naturall, very naturall: Now Pigge, it is a meat, and a meat that is nourishing, and may be long'd for, and so consequently eaten; it may be eaten; very exceeding well eaten: but in the *Fayre,* and as a *Bartholmew*-pig, it cannot be eaten, for the very calling it a *Bartholmew*-pigge, and to eat it so, is a spice of *Idolatry,* and you make the *Fayre,* no better then one of the high *Places.* This I take it, is the state of the question. A high place.[71]

The word "verily" with which Busy begins, though used as almost a meaningless cliché, gives at once his hypocritical answer to the question. But he must translate unacceptable phrases into acceptable ones: the "carnall disease" of longing is a natural longing to eat "a meat that is nourishing." His Puritan terms and his logic (it "may be long'd for, and so consequently eaten") soon lead him to the required conclusion, but he raises a new objection, leaving the question finally in doubt. He will, however, agree to reconsider:

Surely, it may be otherwise, but it is subiect, to construction, subiect, and hath a face of offence, with the weake, a great face, a foule face, but that face may haue a vaile put ouer it, and be shaddowed, as it were, it may be eaten, and in the *Fayre,* I take it, in a Booth, the tents of the wicked. . . .[72]

Used as Busy uses it, jargon has the virtue of concealing an offence from view. The weak, from whom the sight of sin must be hidden, are protected by the edifying rhetoric of a Busy or a Tribulation. Purecraft, like Ananias, is weak in this sense. The

[71] *Ibid.,* I, vi, 39–57 (VI, 37–38).   [72] *Ibid.,* I, vi, 67–72 (VI, 38).

strength of Zeal Busy lies in his utter shamelessness. It is the duty of the strong to give the deed an acceptable name.

Bvs[y]. . . . we may be religious in midst of the prophane, so it be eaten with a reformed mouth, with *sobriety*, and humblenesse; not gorg'd in with gluttony, or greedinesse; there's the feare: for, should she goe there, as taking pride in the place, or delight in the vncleane dressing, to feed the vanity of the eye, or the lust of the palat, it were not well, it were not fit, it were abominable, and not good.[73]

Zeal Busy is a variation of the knavish type among professional classes in Jonson's plays. He is an ignorant hypocrite, as Quarlous says, and he tries to hide both his ignorance and his hypocrisy by the affectation of a religious jargon.

Zeal Busy's language, which is largely composed of cant words and common rhetorical devices, has its most ironical effect when, as often, his actions or his choice of non-Puritan words reveal his hypocrisy. Entering the Fair, he warns his flock against the vanities of the eye and ear. When John asks how they are to find a pig if they do not look about for it, Busy replies:

. . . your mother, religiously wise, conceiueth it may offer it selfe, by other meanes, to the sense, as by way of steeme, which I thinke it doth, here in this place (Huh, huh) yes, it doth. And it were a sinne of obstinacy, great obstinacy, high and horrible obstinacy, to decline, or resist the good titillation of the famelick sense, which is the smell. Therefore be bold (huh, huh, huh) follow the sent. Enter the Tents of the vncleane, for once, and satisfie your wiues frailty. Let your fraile wife be satisfied: your zealous mother and my suffering selfe, will also be satisfied.[74]

This language which pretends to give to eating the sanction of religious authority is accompanied by the stage direction: "*Busy sents after it like a Hound.*" The pretense is maintained by the use of cant words like "religiously wise," "obstinacy," "Tents of the vncleane," "suffering," and the stock rhetorical figures

---

[73] *Ibid.*, I, vi, 72–79 (VI, 38).   [74] *Ibid.*, III, ii, 78–87 (VI, 64).

among Puritans. Busy's indulgence in sensuous experience is also demonstrated by the particular vividness of some of his expressions. It is only after he has partaken of pig that he begins to rail on the wickedness of the "foule *Faire*." He has come, he says,

> To protest against the abuses of it, the foule abuses of it, in regard of the afflicted Saints, that are troubled, very much troubled, exceedingly troubled, with the opening of the merchandize of *Babylon* againe, & the peeping of *Popery* vpon the stals, here, here, in the high places. See you not *Goldylocks*, the purple strumpet, there? in her yellow gowne, and greene sleeues? the prophane pipes, the tinckling timbrells? A shop of reliques![75]

The descriptive words, "yellow," "greene," "tinckling," would scarcely have been used by one who did not look, and had stopped his ears with his fingers.[76]

Adam Overdo, the reforming justice in *Bartholomew Fair*, has a language as distinctive as that of Zeal Busy. A member of the legal profession, he seems to have learned as a judge to affect a style of pompous exhortation. He uses rhetorical habits acquired on the bench even in addressing himself; his project of a visit to the Fair, and the "tragical" consequences of it, are due in large part to the self-deception which he carries out by addressing himself rhetorically. With the exception of the cant word "enormity," however, his speech is characterized not so much by legal terms as by set phrases and rhetorical sentence patterns. "Enormity," used both by the justice and his wife, appears in the play more than twenty times. Mistress Overdo speaks "like a true Iustice of peace's wife[77] . . . in termes of Iustice, and

---

[75] *Ibid.*, III, vi, 88–96 (VI, 84).

[76] The peculiarly dramatic use of the Puritan jargon in *Bartholomew Fair* and *The Alchemist* is made clear by contrast to a reader of Jonson's masque *Love Restored*. The theme of the masque is the lavish expenditure on the royal entertainment. Plutus, the god of money, "with his phrase and face" disguises as Anticupid, the lover of virtue, and speaks like a Puritan. Although he is a part of the antimasque, and a comic character, his speech is otherwise remarkable for its freshness. The Puritan phrase adds reality to the allegory. Like the language of alchemy used in *Mercury Vindicated*, however, it lacks the immediacy of dramatic speech.

[77] *Bartholomew Fair*, IV, iv, 153–54 (VI, 101).

the Stile of authority." [78] Her speech tends to heighten the effect of Overdo's by emphasizing its easily imitated, characteristic qualities. Overdo's declared purpose is to seek out the "enormities" of the Fair. Enormity, a word which was used in Jonson's time both in legal and moral senses, seems in Overdo's speech to be a legal term which has strong moral connotations. The labeling of his "discoveries" with his catchword only confirms his deception. After the pickpocket does his job, Overdo, who is in disguise, becomes suspected. Mistress Overdo is sure of his guilt, and says ". . . now I see hee is a lewd, and pernicious Enormity: (as Master *Ouerdoo* calls him.)" The justice in an aside makes explicit the comment in the mind of the audience: "Mine owne words turn'd vpon mee, like swords." [79]

Not all of the technical terms found in *Bartholomew Fair* are used as jargon. The legal and hunting terms of Quarlous are characteristic of his speech, but they do not represent an affectation. He seems to draw naturally upon his experience to express his thought. The wit of his invective against Winwife gains strength from his hunting metaphors:

. . . would thou wouldst leaue thy exercise of widdow-hunting once! this drawing after an old reuerend Smocke by the splay-foote: There cannot be an ancient *Tripe* or *Trillibub* i' the Towne, but thou art straight nosing it, and 'tis a fine occupation thou'lt confine thy selfe to, when thou ha'st got one; scrubbing a piece of Buffe, as if thou hadst the perpetuity of *Pannyer-alley* to stinke in; or perhaps, worse, currying a carkasse, that thou hast bound thy selfe to aliue.[80]

Knockhem's terms of horse-coursing are also used most commonly as metaphors, as when he presents the Puritan family to Mooncalf: "These are *Banbury-bloods*, o' the sincere stud, come a pigge-hunting." [81] But unlike Quarlous's few special terms, they pervade all his speech. He seems incapable of varying it

[78] *Ibid.*, IV, iii, 121 (VI, 96).   [79] *Ibid.*, III, v, 205–208 (VI, 78).
[80] *Ibid.*, I, iii, 62–70 (VI, 25).   [81] *Ibid.*, III, ii, 97–98 (VI, 64).

appropriately for the occasion. When he tries to be overheard as praising Win-the-Fight he uses the terms that describe a good horse.

. . . doest thou heare, *Whit?* is't not pitty, my delicate darke chestnut here, with the fine leane head, large fore-head, round eyes, euen mouth, sharpe eares, long necke, thinne crest, close withers, plaine backe, deepe sides, short fillets, and full flankes: with a round belly, a plumpe buttocke, large thighes, knit knees, streight legges, short pasternes, smooth hoofes, and short heeles; should lead a dull honest womans life, that might liue the life of a Lady? [82]

The audience appreciates the incongruity of some of the terms, but the speaker is so naïve that he is hardly conscious of speaking in metaphor. The effect on Win is not indicated in the dialogue, and the speech therefore is not dramatically significant as rhetorical praise. Thus it is unlike the rhetoric of Zeal Busy and Adam Overdo, which is used throughout this play to point the contrasts between appearance and reality.

The jargon of *The Devil Is an Ass* (1616) and *The Staple of News* (1625) is not such as old-fashioned knaves used, like mountebanks and alchemists, or even the Puritans. It is the language of the "projectors" of early seventeenth century economic life. "Remember, What number it is, . . ." Satan says in *The Devil Is an Ass,* "Vnlesse it be a *Vice* of quality, Or fashion, now, they take none from vs." [83] Though some of the projects, like "seruing the whole state with Tooth-picks," are, we are told, "somewhat an intricate *Businesse* to discourse," [84] the modern projectors speak with "an aëry voluble tongue," [85] in different terms from Volpone and Subtle, and in a new tune, but essentially the same language.

Although the rhetorical language of Jonson's last plays is similar to that of the work of his prime, its use as dramatic speech is less effective. Jargon is characteristically used with

[82] *Ibid.,* IV, v, 20–28 (VI, 104).
[83] *The Devil Is an Ass,* I, i, 80–112 (VI, 166–67).
[84] *Ibid.,* IV, ii, 39–40 (VI, 232).   [85] *Ibid.,* III, v, 13 (VI, 223).

effects which are more directly satiric and less dramatic. In *The Staple of News*, Pennyboy Canter uses the terms of various professions in satirical descriptions to prove that "all the whole world are *Canters*." The doctor, soldier, poet, and courtier all speak languages which are "cant" because no one can understand them. Jonson's awareness of changes in the life around him, as he grew older, is illustrated by the description of the courtier's speech. It is no longer characterized by the polite, literary affectations of his early plays, but by the new jargon of "projectors." The typical courtier had become a mediator between the court and the business world, and had learned to exploit his connections to advance his own interests in the monopoly system. Pennyboy Canter treats Fitton, the court emissary, as a politician:

>   . . . With all your *fly-blowne proiects*,
> And lookes-out of the *politicks*, your *shut-faces*,
> And reseru'd *Questions*, and *Answers* that you game with, As
> Is't a *Cleare businesse?* will it *mannage well?*
> *My name* must not be vs'd else. Here, 'twill dash.
> Your *businesse has receiu'd a taint*, giue off,
> I may not *prostitute my selfe*. Tut, tut,
> *That little dust I can blow off*, at pleasure.
> *Here's no such mountaine, yet, i' the whole worke,*
> *But a light purse may leuell.* I will *tyde*
> *This affayre* for you; giue it *freight* and *passage*.
> And such *mynt-phrase*, as 'tis the worst of *canting*,
> By how much it affects the *sense*, it has not.[86]

The courtier and the others whom Pennyboy addresses, far from appreciating his ridicule, are impressed by his learning. Only Picklock, the lawyer, seems to understand the rhetorical nature of special jargons, and Jonson's allegory seems to make him the end of a universal chain of gulls.

>   . . . Tut, I am *Vertumnus*,
> On euery change, or chance, vpon occasion,
> A true *Chamælion*, I can colour for't.
> I moue vpon my axell, like a turne-pike,

[86] *The Staple of News*, IV, iv, 63–75 (VI, 358–59).

> Fit my face to the parties, and become,
> Streight, one of them.[87]

Though Picklock uses the jargon of legal terms fully aware of their value in persuasion, he is in the end caught, as he says, "in mine owne halter." The allegory and the direct moralizing at the end weaken this play as drama.

Despite the success of isolated passages, Jonson's last two comedies, *The New Inn* (1629) and *The Magnetic Lady* (1632), point to a further decline of his powers. The uses of jargon are confused and its earlier effects completely dissipated. When it is used to represent a characteristic speech, as in the early Humor plays, it is not used consistently. And when it is a professional speech, its purpose is often divided between persuasion and allegory. The rich meanings on which dramatic irony depends are therefore blurred.

In the fragment of Jonson's pastoral drama *The Sad Shepherd*,[88] there is no place for the kind of rhetorical jargon which is so characteristic of the language of his comedies. The disguise of Maudlin the witch as Marian depends not on her language but on her physical appearance alone, which she has the power to alter. Her curse is not merely rhetorical, although Clarion refers to it scornfully as a "Devills *Pater noster*." [89] Similarly, the numerous hunting terms and dialect words, and the many special words connected with rural life are not used as terms of rhetoric. But their use by Jonson was apparently no less deliberate than his use of technical terms as jargon. Hunting terms are accumulated just as before he had accumulated other technical words.

> Tuc[k]. Here's *Little Iohn* hath harbord you a Deere,
>   I see by his tackling.
> Io[hn].   And a Hart of ten,

---

[87] *Ibid.*, III, i, 34–39 (VI, 327).

[88] The late date of this play has been questioned, but W. W. Greg points out that "there is no definite evidence to oppose to the first line of the prologue and the allusion in Falkland's elegy, which agree in placing it in the few years preceding Jonson's death" (*Ben Jonson's Sad Shepherd*, Louvain, 1905, p. xx).

[89] *The Sad Shepherd*, II, vi, 59 (VII, 36).

I trow hee be, Madam, or blame your men:
For by his Slot, his Entries, and his Port,
His Frayings, Fewmets, he doth promise sport,
And standing 'fore the Dogs; hee beares a head,
Large, and well beam'd: with all rights somm'd, and
 spred.[90]

The audience is not expected, however, to be critical of John's use of this language. The words are used by him unaffectedly. J. W. Fortescue has suggested that Jonson himself is probably guilty here of some affectation.[91] Most technical terms in Jonson's plays are used as a specialized jargon, and as such they have a real dramatic significance when they appear. Their effect within a dramatic context is rhetorical, and is almost independent of a strictly technical meaning. In *The Sad Shepherd*, on the other hand, technical terms are used to fill in the background of rural life, and they have no relation, as words, to the dramatic action. Their intended effect can be most fully appreciated by the audience which understands their technical significance.

The study of Jonson's use of jargon which has filled the last two chapters has illustrated the use of "mere words" in the pattern and technique of his plays. Such language, a "hotchpotch giberidge," as Marston calls it, was a part of the Elizabethan consciousness. In *The Scourge of Villainy*, Marston speaks of

    This affectation,
To speake beyond mens apprehension,
How Apish tis. When all in fusten sute
Is cloth'd a huge *nothing*, all for repute
Of profound knowledge, whē profoūdnes knowes
There's nought cōtaind, but only seeming showes.[92]

---

[90] *Ibid.*, I, ii, 9–15 (VII, 12).

[91] "No man," he writes, "who knew anything of harbouring would have adduced all the possible signs of woodcraft in reference to a single deer, for it is most unusual to encounter all of them on one day. The frayings indeed occur but once a year. Moreover, there was no occasion for all these tokens, for Jonson's harbourer had seen the stag with his eyes" ("Hunting," *Shakespeare's England*, 2 vols., Oxford, 1916, II, 338).

[92] John Marston, *The Scourge of Villanie*, ed. G. B. Harrison, pp. 95–96.

It is because it was part of the Elizabethan consciousness that Jonson could use this language as he does for dramatic purposes. And he was not alone among Elizabethan dramatists in using it. Shakespeare uses it, for example, in *Love's Labour's Lost*. Chapman uses it in minor parts of nearly all his comedies.[93] In *Jack Drum's Entertainment*, Master Puff is described as one who has "a perpetuitie of complement," [94] and both he and John Ellis use ridiculous affectations of speech. In *What You Will*, Marston makes Simplicius speak in terms which recall Jonson's "comical satires": "I shall so ravish her with my court-ship, I have such a variety of discourse, such coppy of phrase to begin, as this; sweete Lady *Ulisses* Dog after his Maisters ten yeares travell, I shall so ticle her, or thus, Pure beauty there is a stone—." [95] In *The Dutch Courtezan*, Caqueteur is described as one whose "discourse is like the long word, *Honorificabilitu-dinitatibus*: a great deale Of sound and no sense." [96] Mistress Mulligrub is an admirer of a "fine terme." [97] In some of these plays, Marston and Chapman were probably influenced by Jonson directly. Yet, unlike Jonson, they use this language only in minor parts of a play among minor characters. As they use it, it could easily become monotonous. The uses of the language in Jonson are so varied that it never seems monotonous. The development from its place in ironic characterization to an important place in dramatic plot, when its ironic effect is richer, is not paralleled in Marston, Chapman, or Shakespeare. It is common throughout Elizabethan drama for foolish characters to speak affectedly, to fail in the observance of decorum, and thus betray their vanity. But Jonson alone has fully developed the dramatic use of the "darke, and obscure termes"

[93] A doctor and a notary, for example, use learned terms of their respective professions in *All Fools* (III, i, 407–16; IV, i, 305–32. In *Plays and Poems of George Chapman: the Comedies*, ed. T. M. Parrott, London, 1914, pp. 140, 149–50). In *May-Day* Quintiliano, and in *The Gentleman Usher* Poggio and Sarpego, are only some of the other characters who use terms affectedly.

[94] *Plays of John Marston*, ed. H. Harvey Wood (3 vols., Edinburgh and London, 1939), III, 191.

[95] *Ibid.*, II, 287–88. [96] *Ibid.*, II, 129. [97] *Ibid.*, II, 107.

which "Professors" hypocritically affect in the attempt to conceal their ignorance, and to prey upon the folly of their dupes. This language conceals the truth from foolish characters on the stage, but not from the audience. Its use by Jonson in his mature plays can be looked upon as a development of the disguise convention, which is so productive of comic irony in Shakespeare. The convention is made to seem less artificial than in Shakespeare, because the language imitates a permanent and common quality of men's speech. What exposes the folly of Epicure Mammon is not a mechanical trick. By working on the vices of his mind, the jargon of Subtle and Face makes him expose his own folly. Thus jargon becomes an integral part of the action, and produces or enhances dramatic irony. It is not merely a "realistic touch" for which a critic of Jonson need apologize,[98] but rather a dramatic technique which may appeal to a modern audience interested in demagogy, advertising, or semantics, as much as to the Elizabethan trained in rhetoric. No other Elizabethan writer experimented so much as Jonson with such language, or produced with it such a variety of dramatic effects.

[98] Gregory Smith writes of *The Alchemist:* "The wealth of detail, all the 'crosslets, crucibles, and cucurbites' of alchemical quackery, is handled with ease. If this is disturbing to the modern, and, to his mind, perhaps the damning of the play, it supplies the realistic touch which Jonson's art demanded and James's London could enjoy" (*Ben Jonson,* London, 1919, p. 114).

CHAPTER VI

HYPERBOLE IN ELIZABETHAN DRAMA AND IN JONSON'S EARLIER PLAYS

HYPERBOLE IS a way of speaking that is not to be understood literally, says *The New English Dictionary;* it is "used to express strong feeling or produce a strong impression." The term was so understood by the Elizabethans. Puttenham defines it as the figure used "when we speake in the superlative and beyond the limites of credit." He describes its value in rhetorical speech as well as the danger of misusing it:

> . . . this maner of speach is vsed, when either we would greatly aduaunce or greatly abase the reputation of any thing or person, and must be vsed very discreetly, or els it will seeme odious, for although a prayse or other report may be allowed beyōd credit, it may not be beyōd all measure, specially in the proseman.[1]

Translating from Vives in *Discoveries,* Jonson expresses a similar thought: "Superlation, and overmuchnesse amplifies. It may be above faith, but never above a meane." Unfortunately, he does not consider its special place in dramatic writing any more than Puttenham. After quoting an example from Virgil, he follows Seneca the Elder in commenting that Virgil "doth not say it was so, but seem'd to be so." He might even more easily have justified a dramatist's use of such exaggeration, because it is not the poet who is supposed to speak at all, but one of his dramatic characters. A character may intentionally be made guilty of excess in speech, and the audience made aware of it.[2] This

---

[1] *Arte of English Poesie,* ed. Gladys Doidge Willcock and Alice Walker (Cambridge, England, 1936), p. 192.

[2] David Worcester (*Art of Satire,* Cambridge, Mass., 1940, p. 24), in examining the effect of a highly exaggerated curse in Rabelais, notes that "the histrionic division of the writer's personality" is partly responsible for it. Jonsonian exaggeration also depends upon its dramatic quality for its effect.

awareness in the audience is especially characteristic of Jonson's plays, and is largely responsible for the effects of Jonsonian hyperbole. Its effects are quite different from those commonly achieved in Elizabethan drama. No other Elizabethan dramatist seems so intent as Jonson to make the audience conscious of the rhetoric being employed, and to use this consciousness for dramatic effect. The early Elizabethan dramatists used hyperbole as a simple convention for expressing strong feeling. In one tradition of the drama, the convention seems to lose its artificiality and to disappear; actually, it is only concealed by art. In another tradition, represented by Jonson's plays, the convention, far from seeming to disappear, is so exaggerated that the audience is made sensitive to its presence. This difference can be defined best by illustrating the uses of hyperbole in some of the dramatists outside of Jonson, and then by studying its appearance in Jonson's plays.

In *The Spanish Tragedy*, hyperbole is used as a convention for expressing strong feeling or producing a strong impression. There is nothing peculiarly dramatic in its expression. The attitude of detachment in the audience, which seems so important in Jonson, is never created. Hyperbole, like other rhetorical figures in the play, is rather ornamental than dramatic. When Hieronimo discovers his son dead, he cries out:

> What sauadge monster, not of humane kinde,
> Hath heere beene glutted with thy harmeles blood,
> And left thy bloudie corpes dishonoured heere,
> For me amidst these darke and deathfull shades,
> To drowne thee with an ocean of my teares?
> O heauens, why made you night to couer sinne?
> By day this deede of darkenes had not beene.
> O earth, why didst thou not in time deuoure
> The vilde prophaner of this sacred bower? [3]

Spoken by a character with whom the audience should sympathize, this speech is intended to convey genuine and deep feel-

---

[3] Thomas Kyd, *The Spanish Tragedy*, II, v, 19–27. All references are to *The Works of Thomas Kyd*, ed. F. S. Boas (Oxford, 1901).

ing. But the verse is so formal that the emotion is never realized. The figures of hyperbole are conventional in themselves, and are not vitalized by any new use. The image of drowning his son who is already dead is quite out of place here; it is introduced as a well-known figure to describe great weeping, but is not to be recognized by the audience as a poorly used rhetorical commonplace. The animal epithet in the first line, and the apostrophes to heaven and to earth in the last lines, are also such as might have been learned from a practical rhetoric book. The audience, however, was expected to accept these figures naïvely. That is, it was not prepared in any way by the dramatist to expect the rhetoric and to discount it.

During his career as an actor, Jonson himself probably played the part of Hieronimo, and in his plays he frequently quotes from *The Spanish Tragedy* with an implication that he disapproved of its rhetoric. In *Every Man in His Humor*, Matthew admires the conceits of the speech beginning, "Oh eies, no eies, but fountains fraught with teares," [4] which Jonson apparently felt as artificial and pointless. Though Jonson turns the speech to his own dramatic purpose, its rhetoric serves none in its original context. "Fountains fraught with teares" was never intended as a vivid, pointed image; its artificiality is emphasized by the pattern of the whole line, which is paralleled three times in the speech. The alliteration is another characteristic ornament, likely to turn up in any passage of hyperbole in the play. For example:

> Where shall I run to breath abroad my woes,
> My woes, whose weight hath wearied the earth?
>
> . . .
>
> Made mountains marsh with spring tides of my teares,
> And broken through the brazen gates of hell. [5]

Alliteration here contributes little to the force of the hyperbole. It remains mere ornament. Jonson's attitude toward rhetoric of this kind is significant. In his earlier plays, in which literary

---

[4] *The Spanish Tragedy*, III, ii, 1.   [5] *Ibid.*, III, vii, 1–2, 8–9.

satire is common, it is frequently ridiculed. In *Poetaster*, for instance, a stage player gives examples of "king DARIVS dolefull straine," "an amorous vaine," and the speech of the "horrible fierce Souldier"; some of these have been identified in early Elizabethan plays. Jonson took slight liberties with the original text to sharpen his satire. For example, in the speech from *The Spanish Tragedy* beginning

> *O, shee is wilder, and more hard, withall,*
> *Then beast, or bird, or tree, or stonie wall,*[6]

he has suppressed a few lines, the omission of which makes the artificial hyperbole stand out. Jonson may have written the lines of the "horrible fierce Souldier" himself since they are unidentified:

> *What? will I braue thee? I, and beard thee too.*
> *A* roman *spirit scornes to beare a braine,*
> *So full of base pusillanimitie.*[7]

The blundering rhythm as well as the diction makes this an effective parody. The rhetorical questions, of which the second apparently repeats one previously asked, betray weakness and fear, and almost amount to a negative answer. The metrical pause at the end of the second line, emphasized by a comma, makes the sense of that line seem complete in itself,[8] and also makes the third line seem to refer back rather to "*A* roman *spirit*" than to "braine," as the speaker apparently intended. Regarding Jonson's attitude toward the characteristic hyperbole of the early Elizabethan plays, one may also recall the reference in *Discoveries* to "the *Tamerlanes,* and *Tamer-Chams* of the late Age, which had nothing in them but the *scenicall* strutting,

---

[6] *Poetaster,* III, iv, 215–16 (*Ben Jonson,* ed. C. H. Herford, Percy and Evelyn Simpson, 10 vols., Oxford, 1925– , IV, 252). All references to Jonson's plays are to this edition. Volume and page are given in parentheses immediately following the citation.

[7] *Poetaster,* III, iv, 224–26 (IV, 252).

[8] The more so because "to bear a brain" was apparently a common idiom; see Chapman's *All Fools,* IV, i, 204 (*Plays and Poems of George Chapman: the Comedies,* ed. T. M. Parrott, London, 1914, p. 146).

and furious vociferation, to warrant them to the ignorant gap-
ers." [9] The attitude here expressed is similar to that implied in
the literary satire of his own early comedies.

Whoever made the additions to *The Spanish Tragedy* used
rhetorical figures more effectively than in the original play, yet
not like Jonson in his undisputed work:

> O God,
> Confusion, mischiefe, torment, death and hell,
> Drop all your stinges at once in my cold bosome,
> That now is stiffe with horror; kill me quickely:
> Be gracious to me, thou infective night,
> And drop this deede of murder downe on me;
> Gird in my wast of griefe with thy large darkenesse,
> And let me not suruiue, to see the light
> May put me in the minde I had a sonne.[10]

The heightened feeling here is expressed not merely by the diction of conventional hyperbole; the diction is given vital and
effective support by a movement which seems natural to a state
of excitement. The rhythmical effects are apparently studied:
the break in the third line, the contrast of the fourth with what
precedes and follows, probably made the speech effective when
declaimed on the stage. As in other parts of the play, however,
the exaggeration is used simply to express strong feelings with
which the audience is expected to sympathize. The play represents reality and the characters in it real individuals. The feelings of the audience are closely associated with those of the
dramatic persons. In the mature plays of Jonson, the audience
is emotionally detached, the play remains a play, and the characters represent a peculiar kind of reality.

While there is a marked contrast between the rhetoric of a
play like *The Spanish Tragedy* and the more sophisticated rhetoric of Jonson, the art of Jonson seems partly anticipated in another writer of rhetorical tragedy, Christopher Marlowe. In
examining Shakespeare's rhetoric, Walter Schirmer distin-

[9] *Discoveries*, in *Ben Jonson*, ed. Herford and Simpson, VIII, 587.
[10] *The Spanish Tragedy*, II, 5 additions, (88)–(96).

guishes two kinds of rhetorical tragedy. In the first, as in *The Spanish Tragedy*, one finds declamatory speeches unrelated to the dialogue, Senecan horrors, and stylized speech-combats in stychomythia. The other type, according to Schirmer, is that in which the basis of the conflict arises from intrigue of which eloquence is the bearer.[11] It is better represented by Marlowe than Kyd. Although Marlowe represents Baldock in *Edward II* as "that smooth-tongu'd scholar," he scarcely touches in that play upon the dramatic possibilities of such a character. Barabas, however, though not explicitly represented as an artful user of language, practices deceit with the aid of rhetoric in a few scenes. The audience is made aware of his purpose in such an aside as: "*Now will I show myself to have more of the serpent than the dove; that is, more knave than fool.*" [12] The effect is to create an attitude of detachment in the audience. There is an understanding between the author and his audience that a character is using language for some persuasive purpose. While this is usual in Jonson, it appears in Marlowe primarily in *The Jew of Malta*, and is not found in Kyd at all. Jonson's leading characters are almost always "acting," and therefore speak rhetoric appropriately.

The First Part of *Tamburlaine*, like *The Spanish Tragedy*, is rich in rhetorical figures. A tendency toward well-rounded speeches of considerable length rather than natural swift dialogue gives many opportunities for rhetorical amplification. The prayer of the Virgins in Act V is a persuasive speech extending over thirty-one lines, in which they plead for Tamburlaine's mercy.[13] Tamburlaine making love speaks fifty-seven lines without interruption.[14] Though common in both of these speeches, hyperbole is only a part of the whole rhetorical struc-

[11] "Shakespeare und die Rhetorik," *Shakespeare-Jahrbuch*, LXXI (1935), p. 18.

[12] *The Jew of Malta*, II, iii, 36–37. All references are to the edition of H. S. Bennett, in *The Jew of Malta and The Massacre at Paris* (London, 1931).

[13] *Tamburlaine the Great*, ed. U. M. Ellis-Fermor (London, 1930), Part I, V, ii, 11–42. All references are to this edition.

[14] *Ibid.*, V, ii, 72–129.

ture, and as hyperbole, it serves no dramatic purpose. Its function is simply to express strong feelings and to create strong
impressions. Though it is not to be understood literally, its exaggeration is not called to the attention of the audience, nor is
there any implication of irony. Most of the hyperbole in the
play is like this. A brief speech may be quoted to illustrate a
well-known characteristic of Marlowe:

> Nay, could their numbers countervail the stars,
> Or ever drizzling drops of April showers,
> Or withered leaves that autumn shaketh down,
> Yet would the Soldan by his conquering power
> So scatter and consume them in his rage,
> That not a man should live to rue their fall.[15]

The comparisons in the first lines, like hyperbole in *The Spanish
Tragedy*, were not intended to impress the audience by their
extravagance, but to be moving.

In other speeches of *Tamburlaine*, however, hyperbole is
used differently. In Act III, when Argydas and Zenocrate dis-
cuss the merits of Tamburlaine, the audience is made aware of
the hyperbole by its contrast with what comes before:

> ARGYD. How can you fancy one that looks so fierce,
> Only disposed to martial stratagems?
> Who, when he shall embrace you in his arms,
> Will tell how many thousand men he slew;
> And, when you look for amorous discourse,
> Will rattle forth his facts of war and blood,
> Too harsh a subject for your dainty ears.
> ZEN. As looks the sun through Nilus' flowing stream,
> Or when the Morning holds him in her arms,
> So looks my lordly love, fair Tamburlaine;
> His talk much sweeter than the Muses' song
> They sung for honour 'gainst Pierides,
> Or when Minerva did with Neptune strive;
> And higher would I rear my estimate
> Than Juno, sister to the highest god,
> If I were matched with mighty Tamburlaine.[16]

[15] *Ibid.*, IV, i, 31–36. [16] *Ibid.*, III, ii, 40–55.

This deliberate contrast between words which debase—"martial stratagems," "rattle forth"—and words which build up the character of Tamburlaine, may make the audience aware of the presence of hyperbole. But Zenocrate is the heroine, and there is no suggestion that her language is too extravagant. The audience is similarly made attentive to language when, earlier in the play, Tamburlaine speaks aside: "Techelles, women must be flattered." [17] Such consciousness on the part of the audience of this play, however, does not create a critical attitude; rhetorical hyperbole is accepted in conventional lyric outbursts. But the situation of Marlowe's audience is nearer to that of Jonson's than to Kyd's. In Act II, Meander taking leave says:

> Your majesty shall shortly have your wish,
> And ride in triumph through Persepolis.

Tamburlaine himself is made to take notice of the effective suggestion of the line; he repeats it:

> And ride in triumph through Persepolis!
> Is it not brave to be a king, Techelles?
> Usumcasane and Theridamas,
> Is it not passing brave to be a king,
> And ride in triumph through Persepolis? [18]

The art of the language has an effect on Tamburlaine which is dramatically important.

But although rhetoric and hyperbole were thus called to the attention of the audience of *Tamburlaine*, they are used straightforwardly and freely in scenes which demand the expression of strong feelings. In fact, hyperbole is used so lavishly toward the end of the play that the audience's emotions are strained to the breaking point. From the scene in which Bejazeth and Zabina curse Tamburlaine and dash their heads against their cages, through the wailings of Zenocrate over the horrible fate of her country, almost to the end of the play, the audience is kept at what seems to us an unbearably high tension of feeling.[19] The

[17] *Ibid.*, I, ii, 107.   [18] *Ibid.*, II, v, 48–54.
[19] *Ibid.*, V, ii, 151–416.

feeling is tense because the audience associates itself with the leading characters. The strain thus put upon the audience sometimes found relief, as the Elizabethan drama developed, in the convention of a comic subplot. In Jonson, however, although hyperbole is still extremely common, the strain is broken completely by creating in the audience an attitude of detachment. Extravagant expression can be contemplated as such. If deep feelings are expressed, they arouse no sympathy in the audience.

T. S. Eliot suggests in his essay on Marlowe that the extravagant speeches of *The Jew of Malta* may be best taken as a kind of farce. A comparison of Marlowe's hyperbole in *Tamburlaine* and in *The Jew of Malta* may be interesting in the light of his suggestion.

Before considering the use of hyperbole in *The Jew of Malta*, certain characteristics of the play as a whole should be recalled. Unlike any other hero of Marlowe's plays, Barabas is a villain. Neither pity nor terror is felt at his "tragic" end. But furthermore, there are no important "good" characters with whom the audience can sympathize; consequently, the actions and speeches of Barabas are sometimes followed with neither sympathy nor antipathy. In addition, the plot of *The Jew of Malta* is based upon Machiavellian intrigue; certain characters deliberately practice deceit of which the audience is always aware. In Act I, Barabas sends his daughter to the nunnery occupying his house, instructing her to "Entreat 'em fair, and give them friendly speech." [20] In Act IV, he himself uses dissembling language to convince the Friars of his conversion to Christianity.[21] Throughout the play the aside is frequently used to make clear to the audience what is being dissembled and what not. As a result, the character sees himself in a dramatic light, and the audience is attentive to rhetorical exaggeration when it is used. The rhetoric neither expresses strong feeling nor produces a strong impression, except as effective

[20] *The Jew of Malta*, I, ii, 286.   [21] *Ibid.*, IV, i, 49–115.

persuasion. These characteristics of the play inevitably produce situations more like those of a Jonsonian comedy of intrigue than of *Tamburlaine* or *Edward II.*

The hyperbole of *The Jew of Malta* is sometimes indistin-
guishable from that of *Tamburlaine:*

> But rather let the brightsome heavens be dim,
> And nature's beauty choke with stifling clouds,
> Than my fair Abigail should frown on me.[22]

This type of comparison with epic associations is characteristic
of Marlowe, and there seems no reason to suppose that here the
audience is not to accept it as expressive of genuine feeling.
With passages like this in mind, one will be cautious in accept-
ing as farce any of the exaggerated language of the play. But
hyperbole has a different effect in other dramatic situations. In
the passage beginning,

> As for myself, I walk abroad nights
> And kill sick people groaning under walls,[23]

the effect is different because the audience is made aware that
both Barabas and Ithamore are indulging in boasts by exaggerating their villainous deeds. These words are not shocking as they
might be if they were not understood as rhetoric. Their rhetorical quality is strictly relevant to the drama. So also in Act IV,
when Barabas catalogues his great wealth for Friar Jacomo and
Friar Bernardine, rhetoric is used with dramatic effect. Barabas
pretends to be newly converted to Christianity. A comic situation is created when the two Friars begin to rival one another in
flattery, hoping to win the Jew's wealth for their respective
houses. Barabas's catalogue is exaggerated for his persuasive
purpose, and it is known to be so by the audience. Picturing this
superabundance of wealth and goods by a method not unlike
Jonson's, Marlowe has written a rhetorical speech of real dramatic significance:

> Cellars of wine, and sollars full of wheat,
> Warehouses stuff'd with spices and with drugs,

---

[22] *Ibid.,* II, iii, 331-33. Cf. *ibid.,* II, i, 1-6.   [23] *Ibid.,* II, iii, 175-76.

Whole chests of gold, in bullion, and in coin,
Besides, I know not how much weight in pearl,
Orient and round, have I within my house; . . .
In Florence, Venice, Antwerp, London, Seville,
Frankfort, Lubeck, Moscow, and where not,
Have I debts owing.[24]

There are other scenes in this play which seem clearly to indicate that Marlowe was conscious of discovering new uses for
rhetoric. In Act IV, the courtezan Bellamira and Pilia Borza
have a plot under hand to get the Jew's wealth through the help
of his villainous Turk, Ithamore. Bellamira pretends to be in
love with Ithamore, invites him to her house and flatters him.
Ithamore is represented as practically speechless at first, and
makes a number of extraordinary blunders. (Later in the scene
Pilia Borza says ironically, "You'd make a rich poet, sir.") But
at one point in the scene, when Ithamore is left alone with
Bellamira, he regains his composure and makes love in the best
rhetorical manner:

BELL.   I have no husband, sweet, I'll marry thee.
ITHA.   Content, but we will leave this paltry land,
And sail from hence to Greece, to lovely Greece.
I'll be thy Jason, thou my golden fleece:
Where painted carpets o'er the meads are hurl'd,
And Bacchus' vineyards overspread the world:
Where woods and forests go in goodly green,
I'll be Adonis, thou shalt be Love's Queen.
The meads, the orchards, and the primrose-lanes.
Instead of sedge and reed, bear sugar-canes:
Thou in those groves, by Dis above,
Shalt live with me, and be my love.[25]

As H. S. Bennett points out in his edition, Marlowe has here
written lines in the manner of *The Passionate Shepherd*, and
has put them in the mouth of a thoroughly naïve comic character. The attention of the audience is thus directed to the language, which is used to express with irony the height of feeling
to which Ithamore has been moved. Ithamore does not use hy-

[24] *Ibid.*, IV, i, 66–70, 74–76.   [25] *Ibid.*, IV, iv, 94–105.

perbole consciously, as Barabas did. Mammon in *The Alche-mist* is also unconscious of his use of hyperbole while the audience is made aware of it. One is reminded of Mammon's exaggeration again at the end of the scene. A strong feeling is represented which the audience can observe with critical ob-jectivity:

> BELL. Come my dear love, let's in and sleep together.
> ITHA. O, that ten thousand nights were put in one,
>   That we might sleep seven years together afore we wake.[26]

Later in Act IV another comic situation is intensified by a dra-matic use of hyperbole. Ithamore speaks with his new-found confidence to Barabas, who is in disguise: " 'Tis a strange thing of that Jew, he lives upon pickled grasshoppers and sauced mushrumbs." [27] This language is paralleled in *Volpone* when Mosca, pretending Volpone is deaf, encourages Corvino to give free rein to his insults.[28] Marlowe got dramatic effects from hyperbole in *The Jew of Malta* unlike any in *Tamburlaine*, and he was not unconscious of them. If he began with the intention of writing a popular tragedy of blood, the situations them-selves, which grew out of the plot of intrigue, suggested the new uses to which hyperbole is put.

While Jonson may be said to develop and refine some of the rhetorical qualities of *The Jew of Malta*, Shakespeare seems rather to begin with rhetorical qualities more like those of *Tam-burlaine*, and to develop an art, as Schirmer observes,[29] which conceals rhetoric. In Shakespeare the emphasis is on what is said; often, in Jonson, the dramatic effect depends much more upon how it is said. Hyperbole is used in the early plays of Shakespeare, as in *Tamburlaine*, for the expression of strong feeling. In *Richard III*, for example, Queen Elizabeth laments in these terms:

---

[26] *Ibid.*, IV, iv, 139–41.　　　　[27] *Ibid.*, IV, vi, 62.
[28] *Volpone*, I, v, 51–65 (V, 42–43).
[29] "Shakespeare und die Rhetorik," *Shakespeare-Jahrbuch*, LXXI (1935), p. 16.

> All springs reduce their currents to mine eyes,
> That I, being govern'd by the watery moon,
> May send forth plenteous tears to drown the world.
> Ah for my husband, for my dear lord Edward! [30]

The commonplace nature of the complaint is obvious from the metaphor of drowning the world with tears; moreover, the words by which these lines are introduced define their formal nature explicitly:

> Give me no help in lamentation;
> I am not barren to bring forth complaints.

And yet, conventional as it is,[31] the language is to be accepted by the audience as an expression of real feeling which demands sympathy. Because such language is used by "good" characters, it is not likely to be suspect when it is also used by such an intriguer as Richard himself. When, speaking of his father, he tells Elizabeth, "thy scorns drew'st rivers from his eyes," [32] the hyperbole cannot be understood ironically to suggest the untruthfulness of his argument. In Shakespeare's mature plays, hyperbole continues to appear as an expression of strong feeling with which the audience is to sympathize, although its form exhibits a greater freedom of invention.

> Had I as many eyes as thou hast wounds,
> Weeping as fast as they stream forth thy blood,
> It would become me better than to close
> In terms of friendship with thine enemies.[33]

Thus Antony addresses the corpse of Caesar. Again, a Gentleman in *The Winter's Tale* describes as follows the meeting of Leontes and Polixenes, after Leontes had discovered his lost daughter: "There might you have beheld one joy crown another, so and in such manner, that it seem'd sorrow wept to take leave of them; for their joy waded in tears." [34] Although this is

---

[30] *Richard III*, II, ii, 68-71.
[31] Another suggestion of the traditionally rhetorical nature of this tragedy is the formal discussion of rhetoric, IV, iv, 116-35.
[32] *Richard III*, I, iii, 176. [33] *Julius Caesar*, III, i, 200-203.
[34] *The Winter's Tale*, V, ii, 47-51.

a description, not a direct expression of strong feeling, it represents Shakespearean hyperbole in its maturity. Embedded deep in metaphor, it has a peculiar force because of its rich suggestiveness. "Tears to drown the world" has one simple meaning, but "their joy waded in tears" has more. To suggest through metaphor the difficulty and slowness with which they realized their joy is richer and subtler than merely to say they wept tears enough "to drown the world."

Even in his early plays, as Schirmer points out, Shakespeare uses rhetorical speech not only as a conventional expression of real feeling, but also often as the basis for the growth of a plot of intrigue.[35] But the speech of these intriguing characters is not made immediately recognizable to the audience as rhetoric. In an opening soliloquy of *Richard III*, Gloucester explains his villainous plots. He warns the audience at once that he is "subtle, false, and treacherous," and throughout the play he comments on his own speech. At one point he explains:

> I'll in, to urge his hatred more to Clarence,
> With lies, well steel'd with weighty arguments.[36]

Later in describing his speech, he again uses the Elizabethan convention of a direct address to the audience:

> But then I sigh, and, with a piece of Scripture,
> Tell them that God bids us do good for evil;
> And thus I clothe my naked villany
> With odd old ends stol'n forth of holy writ,
> And seem a saint when most I play the devil.[37]

When the rhetoric here described is illustrated, however, it is distinguished not by elaborate stylistic devices—these appear in the speeches of all characters—but by simple dissembling. Gloucester tells his enemies, Rivers and Grey:

---

[35] Walter Schirmer, "Shakespeare und die Rhetorik," *Shakespeare-Jahrbuch*, LXXI (1935), p. 18.

[36] *Richard III*, I, i, 147–48.

[37] *Ibid.*, I, iii, 334–38. Other references to artful speech in this play are I, ii, 168; I, iii, 347–52; III, i, 82–83; III, v, 95–97; III, vii, 18–22; IV, iv, 154.

> I do not know that Englishman alive
> With whom my soul is any jot at odds
> More than the infant that is born to-night.
> I thank my God for my humility.[38]

Similarly, when he woos Anne, whose husband he has murdered, his method of persuasion is simple flattery. It is what he says, not his style, that has dramatic significance. In Jonson this precedence is reversed. Jonson's audience is not only told of the dissembling nature of particular characters, but the qualities of their speech are constantly illustrated, and pointed to in asides and comments of other characters. Shakespeare's audience, on the other hand, is left more to its own resources, and permitted to become involved in the action with emotional sympathies or antipathies. When there are allusions to the stage in Shakespeare, the play in which they appear represents real life; in Jonson the play is usually treated as a play. This contrast between Shakespeare's and Jonson's methods is clear to the reader of *Measure for Measure*, which is almost exactly contemporary with *Volpone*. When Claudio is imprisoned for the seduction of Juliet, he sends Lucio to ask his sister to go

> To the strict deputy; bid herself assay him.
> I have great hope in that; for in her youth
> There is a prone and speechless dialect,
> Such as move men. Beside, she hath prosperous art
> When she will play with reason and discourse,
> And well she can persuade.[39]

The innocent Isabel does appear to plead before Angelo, and she speaks without guile. It is her ingenuousness, not her art, that moves Angelo. The interest of the audience is concentrated not on her rhetoric and its effect, but on the truth of her moral argument and the temptation with which Angelo is confronted. Claudio and Lucio had hoped Isabel would employ art in persuasion, and Lucio frequently comments on her speech. His asides, however, only mark the contrast between her purpose

---

[38] *Ibid.*, II, i, 69–72.   [39] *Measure for Measure*, I, ii, 186–91.

and his. Her method of persuasion is artless, and her language apparently natural. The effect of the situation does not depend upon the quality of her language as such. The development of rhetoric in Shakespeare was toward a speech which seems natural for the characters using it. The art of his language takes effect without being noticed. Jonson's method, on the other hand, demands that the rhetorical art used by many characters be noticed. Rhetoric is itself a medium of dramatic expression.

Before examining in detail the use of hyperbole in Jonson's mature plays, however, it is necessary to observe that he sometimes uses exaggerated language differently in his earlier plays and in his tragedies. His uses of hyperbole may be divided into three. It is sometimes a simple conventional expression of strong human emotion; second, it is a conventional expression of the violent, unnatural emotion of symbolic or stylized characters; finally, it is used with various ironic effects, when the audience is made to recognize its rhetorical quality. It is the last, especially developed in *Volpone* and *The Alchemist*, that is characteristic of Jonson's mature comedy. The two earliest plays which we possess in their original form, *The Case Is Altered* and *Every Man in His Humor*, contain hyperbole not unlike that found in other Elizabethan plays already examined: it is exaggerated language to be accepted by the audience as a conventional expression of strong feeling. In *The Case Is Altered* the characters who are treated sympathetically express themselves in such conventional terms; Rachel cries out to Angelo:

> Touch not my body, with those impious hands,
> That like hot Irons seare my trembling heart,
> And make it hisse, at your disloyalty.[40]

Paulo uses similar language in condemning his faithless friend:

> Thou monster, euen the soule of trechery!
> O what dishonord title of reproch,
> May my tongue spit in thy deserued face?
> Me thinkes my very presence should inuert

[40] *The Case Is Altered*, V, viii, 3-5 (III, 177).

> The steeled organs of those traytrous eyes,
> To take into thy heart, and pierce it through.[41]

These speeches are rightly felt to be uncharacteristic of Jonson; he does not in his mature plays use conventional expression so uncritically. Yet in other parts of *The Case Is Altered*, hyperbole is used with ironical effect. In Jaques's formal speeches on the subject of his gold, he uses an elaborate rhetoric with much hyperbole to express sentiments unacceptable to the audience. If Jonson had revised this play for the 1616 Folio, as he did *Every Man in His Humor*, he would probably have eliminated the hyperbole from the speeches quoted of Rachel and Paulo, but would have retained the hyperbole of Jaques:

> O in what golden circle haue I dans't?
> *Millaine* these od'rous and enfloured fields
> Are none of thine, no heres *Elizium*,
> Heere blessed Ghosts do walke, this is the Court
> And glorious palace where the God of gold
> Shines like the sonne, of sparkling maiesty.[42]

These lines have some of the qualities of Volpone's opening soliloquy. When an emotion to which the audience is so unsympathetic is treated in such elevated language, the language has an ironic effect. It is "poetic speech," expressive of a soul "highly strung," [43] but its rich effect as dramatic poetry is due to the interaction between its language and the character and feeling of the speaker.

The revision of *Every Man in His Humor* illustrates how Jonson eliminated certain types of hyperbole in the course of his development as a dramatist, and how he exaggerated others. In the original version, after reading a letter to his son, Lorenzo Senior exclaims:

> The modest paper eene lookes pale for griefe
> To feele her virgin-cheeke defilde and staind
> With such a blacke and criminall *inscription*.[44]

[41] *Ibid.*, V, viii, 43–48 (III, 179).   [42] *Ibid.*, V, iv, 1–6 (III, 172).
[43] See Herford and Simpson, I, 322.
[44] *Every Man in His Humor*, Quarto of 1601, I, i, 186–88 (III, 202).

This conventional rhetoric is completely eliminated from the Folio version. On the other hand, hyperbole is further emphasized in the revision of the jealous Thorello's speech on the power of beauty. The Quarto reads:

> Oh beauty is a *Proiect* of some power,
> Chiefely when oportunitie attends her:
> She will infuse true motion in a stone,
> Put glowing fire in an Icie soule,
> Stuffe peasants bosoms with proud *Cæsars* spleene. . . .[45]

These lines are changed in the Folio to read:

> No beautie, no; you are of too good caract,
> To be left so, without a guard, or open!
> Your lustre too'll enflame, at any distance,
> Draw courtship to you, as a iet doth strawes,
> Put motion in a stone, strike fire from ice,
> Nay, make a porter leape you, with his burden! [46]

The tone is completely changed, the metaphors having been stripped of all noble associations. The hyperbole of the third and fourth lines of the Quarto is concentrated into one line, and, whereas in the original it has a clear metaphorical meaning, in the revision, when "soul" is eliminated, it stands out more clearly as hyperbolical language, "beyond the limits of credit." The Folio version does not eliminate rhetoric of this kind but places it in clearer relief. If only the earlier version is considered with *The Case Is Altered*, it may be said that in Jonson's earliest plays, he most commonly uses hyperbole as a conventional expression of strong human feeling. But even in *The Case Is Altered*, in the speeches of Jaques, such expression is sometimes used to enhance the irony of a dramatic situation. That this is the direction which Jonson later followed is suggested, as we have seen, by the kind of revisions he made in *Every Man in His Humor*.

In *Every Man Out of His Humor*, as O. J. Campbell has shown, Jonson tried to adapt some conventions of formal satire

---

[45] *Ibid.*, III, i, 22–26 (III, 233).
[46] *Ibid.*, Folio of 1616, III, iii, 22–27 (III, 346–47).

to the drama. One of these conventions was the violent speech which the formal satirist permitted himself in castigating his subject.[47] The satirist is represented in Jonson's first "comical satire" by two characters, Asper and Macilente, both of whom express their feelings in hyperbole. In the opening soliloquy, the envious Macilente looks at men around him and reflects:

> When I see these (I say) and view my selfe,
> I wish the organs of my sight were crackt;
> And that the engine of my griefe could cast
> Mine eye-balls, like two globes of wild-fire, forth,
> To melt this vnproportion'd frame of nature.[48]

This language is no less conventional than the hyperbole of *Tamburlaine*. It is offered as an expression of feeling, and its quality as rhetoric is not explicitly drawn to the attention of the audience for a critical rejection of it. The obvious difference between its effect and that of *Tamburlaine* is due to the type of character using it. Here it is the expression of a character whose emotions are not human at all, because he represents more than an individual: he is a dramatic abstraction whose entire action is determined by the humor of envy. He commands neither sympathy nor antipathy from the audience. His language cannot be judged by human standards; if it were more real and less artificial, it would seem less natural. Macilente is no more human than Envy in *Poetaster*, who uses the same kind of language (in the Prologue):

> The *Scene* is, ha!
> ROME? ROME? and ROME? Cracke ey-strings, and your balles
> Drop into earth; let me be euer blind.[49]

T. S. Eliot has observed the special effectiveness of the language of this speech, and he remarks, on the opening speeches of *Poetaster* and *Catiline:* "It is not human life that informs Envy and Sylla's ghost, but it is energy of which human life is only an-

---

[47] O. J. Campbell, *Comicall Satyre and Shakespeare's Troilus and Cressida,* (San Marino, Calif., 1938), p. 61.
[48] *Every Man Out of His Humor,* I, i, 24–28 (III, 442–43).
[49] *Poetaster,* Envy's Prologue, ll. 27–29 (IV, 204).

other variety." [50] The grouping together of *Catiline* and *Poetaster* suggests at once that Jonson in his maturity never completely abandoned the direction he took when he began to write his "comical satires." It is perhaps significant that in 1616 he was willing to publish *Every Man Out of His Humor* with only minor changes, but no earlier play. Thus in the "comical satires" Jonson develops what is called here the second use of hyperbole. It is used to express the unnatural and sometimes violent emotions of his own peculiar and unreal dramatic characters. It serves as a kind of decorum, a mark of character, or rather of a class of characters.

But like other forms of Jonsonian rhetoric, hyperbole is perhaps most characteristic of Jonson when the audience is made aware of its rhetorical and conventional character. The audience is given the role of ironist when in *Cynthia's Revels* Amorphus gives his hat to Asotus as "the *hieroglyphicke* of my affection," and boasts of its virtues:

. . . you shall alter it to what forme you please, it will take any blocke; I haue receiu'd it varied (on record) to the three thousandth time, and not so few: It hath these vertues beside; your head shall not ake vnder it; nor your braine leaue you, without licence; It will preserue your complexion to eternitie; for no beame of the sunne (should you weare it vnder *Zona torrida*) hath power to approach it by two ells. It is proofe against thunder, and inchantment: and was giuen mee by a great man (in Russia) as a especiall-priz'd present; and constantly affirm'd to bee the hat, that accompanied the politike Vlysses, in his tedious, and ten yeeres trauels. [51]

The irony here is dependent upon the audience's superior view of the character, which it can watch with a detached, amused interest. The affectedness of his speech is emphasized by the exaggerated figures of hyperbole. The irony of Jaques's speeches in *The Case Is Altered* depends more upon situation, even though he often speaks in soliloquy. Situation is more im-

[50] *Selected Essays* (London, 1932), p. 151.
[51] *Cynthia's Revels*, I, iv, 185–96 (IV, 60).

portant also in another scene of *Cynthia's Revels,* which appears, however, only in the Folio and may be a late addition. Mercury and Crites ridicule the affectations of the courtiers by joining in their contest and competing with their them in making elaborate rhetorical speeches of compliment. Mercury says:

Sweet Madame, on what part of you soeuer a man casts his eye, he meets with perfection; you are the liuely image of VENVS, throughout; all the GRACES smile in your cheeks; your beautie nourishes, as well as delights; you haue a tongue steep't in honie; and a breath like a panther: your brests and forehead are whiter than gotes milke, or *May*-blossomes; a cloud is not so soft as your skinne.[52]

Mercury's speech is a direct satire on courtly forms of rhetoric. Despite the exaggeration which marks it as parody, it is accounted by the courtiers worthy of a prize. The language is not unlike that used by Sejanus and Volpone in making love, but the fact that it is used merely as a set speech in a contest, and not actually addressed to another dramatic character, makes it less effective dramatically than it will become in Jonson's later plays.

[52] *Ibid.,* V, iv, 429–36 (IV, 152). Crites also uses hyperbole in his more obvious and explicit parody of Hedon (V, iv, 597–606).

CHAPTER VII

THE HYPERBOLE OF JONSON'S MATURE PLAYS

IN WRITING *Sejanus,* Jonson deliberately turned to tragedy, which to him meant in part, "grauity and height of Elocution, fulnesse and frequencie of Sentence." [1] The elevated style of *Sejanus,* however, has much in common with the style of the comedies *Poetaster,* which preceded it, and *Volpone,* which followed. Similarly, the effects of hyperbole in *Sejanus* are parallel to those of *Poetaster,* on the one hand, and of *Volpone,* on the other. In the first place, Jonson often uses hyperbole in *Sejanus* as a conventional expression of strong feeling. However, it is rather like the hyperbole of Envy's Prologue to *Poetaster* than that of *Tamburlaine,* in which the characters and emotions approach reality.

> If I could gesse he had but such a thought,
> My sword should cleaue him downe from head to heart,
> But I would finde it out: and with my hand
> I'ld hurle his panting braine about the ayre,
> In mites, as small as *atomi,* to'vndoe
> The knotted bed—. [2]

Here neither the character using it nor the audience is made especially aware of hyperbole as a rhetorical figure, and it is to be accepted as a convention. Many such oaths and curses of Arruntius, a character treated sympathetically throughout the play, are in hyperbole.

More often, however, the exaggeration has function in mov-

---

[1] *Sejanus,* "To the Readers," ll. 19-20 (*Ben Jonson,* ed. C. H. Herford, Percy and Evelyn Simpson, 10 vols., Oxford, 1925- , IV, 350). All references to Jonson's plays are to this edition. Volume and page are given in parentheses immediately following the citation.

[2] *Ibid.,* I, 253-58 (IV, 363).

ing the action forward, and when it is recognized by the audience as rhetorical, it produces dramatic irony. For example, when Tiberius speaks before the Senate, Arruntius, in asides to the audience, continually draws attention to his dissimulating rhetoric:

> Tib.   My comforts are so flowing in my ioyes,
>   As, in them, all my streames of griefe are lost,
>   No lesse then are land-waters in the sea,
>   Or showres in riuers; though their cause was such,
>   As might haue sprinkled eu'n the gods with teares:
>   Yet since the greater doth embrace the lesse,
>   We couetously obey.
> (Arr.   Well acted, Caesar.) [3]

The dramatic effect is dependent, not merely upon Tiberius's simple untruth, but on its elaborate coloring with hyperbolical figures of speech. In an earlier speech, when Tiberius protests,

> No man, here,
> Receiue our speeches, as *hyperbole's*,[4]

his obvious rhetorical device merely calls attention to itself, and marks the entire speech for the audience as persuasive rhetoric. The audience is made aware of the use of rhetoric in other parts of the play also. When Latiaris attempts to draw treasonous statements from Sabinus, he uses hyperbole and other rhetorical figures to arouse him.[5] The audience is detached and critical, as it is again when Eudemus addresses Livia on Sejanus's behalf:

> Some will thinke
> Your fortune could not yeeld a deeper sound,
> Then mixt with Drvsvs; But, when they shall heare
> That, and the thunder of Seianvs meet,
> Seianvs, whose high name doth strike the starres,
> And rings about the concaue, great Seianvs,
> Whose glories, stile, and titles are himselfe,
> The often iterating of Seianvs:
> They then will lose their thoughts, and be asham'd
> To take acquaintance of them.[6]

---

[3] *Ibid.*, III, 99–105 (IV, 396).   [4] *Ibid.*, I, 532–33 (IV, 372).
[5] *Ibid.*, IV, 158–61 (IV, 423).   [6] *Ibid.*, II, 94–103 (IV, 378).

This scene between Livia and her physician, who advises her on the preservation of her outward beauty, and at the same time corrupts her inwardly, borders on the comic. Eudemus has a function not unlike that of Mosca or Face in Jonson's comedies, and the dramatic effect of his rhetoric is ironic like theirs. When Sejanus uses elaborate rhetorical patterns in making love to Livia, Jonson seems again to anticipate *Volpone*. The speech is preceded by a discussion of the fittest person to poison Livia's husband. When Lygdus is suggested, Sejanus says:

> Send him to me, I'le worke him. Royall ladie,
> Though I haue lou'd you long, and with that height
> Of zeale, and dutie, (like the fire, which more
> It mounts, it trembles) thinking nought could adde
> Vnto the feruour, which your eye had kindled;
> Yet, now I see your wisedome, iudgement, strength,
> Quicknesse, and will, to apprehend the meanes
> To your owne good, and greatnesse, I protest
> My selfe through rarefied, and turn'd all flame
> In your affection. . . .[7]

Livia's willingness to have a part in the murder of her husband has inspired this elaborate and artificial compliment. The audience, always aware that Sejanus's love is merely a political maneuver, is again reminded of his dissembling purpose by the quality of his language.

The last act of *Sejanus* has the tone and effect of Jonsonian comedy. Although Jonson had apparently set out to create characters of dignity, most of them become ridiculous in the last act. A parallel with *The Jew of Malta* suggests itself. Sejanus and Macro are both devoted to Machiavellian policy. The situations which the plots present seem to lead both Marlowe and Jonson from an original tragic intention to writing something like comedy. When Sejanus's plots are about to collapse all around him, and he still buoys up his hopes with ambitious fancy, he no longer seems a dignified tragic hero:

[7] *Ibid.*, II, 24-33 (IV, 375-76).

> My roofe receiues me not; 'tis aire I tread:
> And, at each step, I feele my' aduanced head
> Knocke out a starre in heau'n! [8]

The audience, completely objective and critical, can observe
here the swelling ambition, reflected in hyperbole, which is
about to be pricked and deflated. Sejanus knows he has reason
to fear, and his fawning on Macro, in contrast with his former
insolence, is comic. The audience watches him as he is deceived
into believing that Macro is his friend. The elaboration of his
set speech, not without dramatic value, emphasizes the irony of
his condemnation of fear.

> What base, vncomely things it makes men doe?
> Suspect their noblest friends, (as I did this)
> Flatter poore enemies, intreat their seruants,
> Stoupe, court, and catch at the beneuolence
> Of creatures, vnto whom (within this houre)
> I would not haue vouchsaf'd a quarter-looke,
> Or piece of face? [9]

In *Sejanus*, and to a less extent in earlier plays, some anticipa-
tions of the language of *Volpone* have been observed. But it is in
the latter play that Jonson seems to perfect the use of rhetorical
hyperbole for purposes of comic irony. When it is used, the
audience is made aware of its rhetorical nature; and it is used in
many different situations with various effects. Its uses in *Volpone* may be divided into two. Each represents a situation in
which rhetoric is used as part of the technique of irony. First
are those scenes in which rhetoric calls attention to itself, as in
the speeches of Jaques in *The Case Is Altered*, by expressing an
emotion in conflict with the normal attitude of the audience.
Here it is not pointed out explicitly, but it affects the tone of a
speech. Second are those scenes in which rhetoric is used in deliberate persuasion. These are numerous and varied. For instance, there is the greatest difference in effect between the
persuasive speeches of the knaves, Mosca and Volpone, who

---

[8] *Ibid.*, V, 7–9 (IV, 436).   [9] *Ibid.*, V, 384–90 (IV, 451).

usually understand the effects of their speech, and those of the dupes, especially Corvino and Voltore, who are usually ignorant of the real effects of their speech.

The tone of the opening scene of *Volpone* is set by the rhetorical quality of its language. Volpone addresses his gold as his "*saint*," and Mosca joins him in extravagant praise of the "cunning purchase" of it. Although it is divided between two characters, the entire scene is composed like one speech. The lofty emotion apparently justifies the grand style:

> Good morning to the day; and, next, my gold:
> Open the shrine, that I may see my *saint*.
> Haile the worlds soule, and mine. More glad then is
> The teeming earth, to see the long'd-for sunne
> Peepe through the hornes of the celestial *ram*,
> Am I, to view thy splendor, darkening his; . . .[10]

Critics since Upton have often praised the "tragic sublimity" of this speech.[11] Volpone is said to reveal in it "his appreciation of beauty." [12] The allusions to classical mythology are thought by another critic to soften our normal revulsion.[13] We are supposed to believe upon hearing it that there is poetry in Volpone's soul, and that his covetous and lustful nature has been so refined that it is no longer ugly but noble. These critics seem to neglect the dramatic value of Volpone's "poetry." When such formal and elevated speech is used to praise what the audience feels is unworthy of such praise, the effect is ironic. The quality of language helps to create the tone which is characteristic of the whole play. Volpone's sensuality and its expression may win the interest of the audience, but not its sympathy. The audience remains unmoved. But, like the reader of Erasmus's *Praise of Folly*, it is forced to doubt its own moral position as

[10] *Volpone*, I, i, 1–6 (V, 24–25).

[11] James Upton, *Remarks on Three Plays of Benjamin Jonson* (London, 1749), p. 4; compare J. A. Symonds, *Ben Jonson* (New York, 1886), pp. 73–74.

[12] Henry Ten Eyck Perry, *Masters of Dramatic Comedy* (Cambridge, Mass., 1939), p. 98.

[13] Charles Francis Wheeler, *Classical Mythology in the Plays, Masques, and Poems of Ben Jonson* (Princeton, N.J., 1938), p. 11.

Volpone's arguments are amplified, and he describes the methods of making money which he scorns. As in the mock encomium of Erasmus, rhetoric is used as a vehicle of irony. Although the rhetorical quality of the language may not be pointed out explicitly, as in some situations of the play, the style deepens the ironic sense of the audience. Language is used similarly in Mosca's soliloquy in praise of parasites; [14] and by Volpone, after he has seen Celia at her window:

> . . . angry CVPID, bolting from her eyes,
> Hath shot himselfe into me, like a flame;
> Where, now, he flings about his burning heat,
> As in a fornace, an ambitious fire,
> Whose vent is stopt.[15]

This language in its effect is quite unlike those conventionally rhetorical professions of love which could be illustrated even from Jonson's earlier plays. The rhetorical convention is here used more deliberately, and the emotion which it expresses, as the audience knows, is sheer lust. The grand style is used to point an ironic contrast; the conventional language has been revitalized by giving it a dramatic meaning.

The second and more conspicuous use of hyperbole in *Volpone* is in the many situations which require rhetorical persuasion. When Volpone makes love to Celia, his language is calculated to persuade:

> Thy bathes shall be the iuyce of iuly-flowres,
> Spirit of roses, and of violets,
> The milke of vnicornes, and panthers breath
> Gather'd in bagges, and mixt with *cretan* wines.
> Our drinke shall be prepared gold, and amber; . . .[16]

Jonson is in a sense here "out-Marlowing Marlowe," [17] but with a difference. The audience is fully aware of Volpone's rhetorical aim, and consequently maintains an attitude of detachment.

---

[14] *Volpone*, III, i, 7–33 (V, 66–67).   [15] *Ibid.*, II, iv, 3–7 (V, 58).
[16] *Ibid.*, III, vii, 213–17 (V, 83).
[17] G. Gregory Smith, *Ben Jonson* (London, 1919), p. 110.

This speech is more than a piece of persuasion to Volpone, however. It expresses his deep lust, and, though the emotion may be genuine, the audience is not sympathetic to it. The great exaggeration calls attention to itself, and helps to maintain in the audience the attitude which is essential to Jonson's purpose. The effect of the hyperbole in this speech is partly due to its recognized purpose of persuasion, and partly to the attitude of the audience toward the emotion which it expresses. The fact that Celia remains unmoved by Volpone's advances confirms the audience in its attitude toward Volpone's rhetoric and his emotion.

When hyperbole is used successfully as a means of rhetorical persuasion, the effects which it produces are again different. It may or may not express emotion in the speaker. In describing Corvino's wife to Volpone, Mosca appears to be deeply moved, but the very profusion of comparisons makes the audience aware of the rhetorical purpose of his speech, and suspect that Mosca himself is plotting to trap Volpone. The images are not expected to move the audience so much as to make it observe Mosca's pretended emotion. Similarly, after Voltore, against his own interest, has successfully defended Volpone in court, Mosca praises him in extravagant language:

> I'ld ha' your tongue, sir, tipt with gold, for this;
> I'ld ha' you be the heire to the whole citie;
> The earth I'ld haue want men, ere you want liuing:
> They'are bound to erect your statue, in St. Markes.[18]

Although Mosca has reason to praise him for helping to gull himself, the audience knows that he is also merely flattering him.

In other scenes it is quite clear to the audience that no emotion is involved although hyperbole is used. Its purpose is only persuasion. For example, Mosca uses such language when he receives Volpone's clients in Act I. In answering Voltore's

---

[18] *Volpone*, IV, vi, 64–67 (V, 107).

inevitable question, he humbles himself as a poor dependent
(which in a sense he is):

> VOLT. Am I inscrib'd his heire, for certayne?
> Mos.   Are you?
> I doe beseech you, sir, you will vouchsafe
> To write me, i' your family. All my hopes,
> Depend vpon your worship. I am lost,
> Except the rising sunne doe shine on me.
> VOLT. It shall both shine, and warme thee, MOSCA.
> Mos.   Sir,
> I am a man, that haue not done your loue
> All the worst offices: here I weare your keyes, . . .[19]

Voltore understands Mosca's speech only as a unit, and therefore as an affirmative answer to his question. But the first two
words taken alone merely repeat the question without com-
mitting the speaker. If the next two sentences are taken alone,
they represent a petition which Mosca can make sincerely even
if Voltore is not Volpone's heir. The last sentence, taken alone,
can also be honestly spoken, since Mosca does not actually
identify Voltore as "the rising sunne." Voltore so identifies
himself, however, and in doing so, by continuing Mosca's hyperbole, he gulls himself. Mosca's next speech, beginning with
the figure of litotes, is also ambiguous. In describing Volpone's
hoard as if it were Voltore's, he may simply mean that it represents Voltore's many gifts. The audience, conscious of Mosca's
purpose, must admire the skill by which these meanings are
kept just beyond Voltore's grasp. Mosca is an accomplished
master of language, and there is an additional irony when he
praises lawyers for their ability in speaking:

> That, with most quick agilitie, could turne,
> And re-turne; make knots, and vndoe them;
> Giue forked counsell; take prouoking gold
> On either hand, and put it vp: . . .[20]

The supposed great eloquence of Voltore, which is here observed, will be used later in the play for a dramatically effective

---

[19] *Ibid.*, I, iii, 33–40 (V, 33).   [20] *Ibid.*, I, iii, 56–59 (V, 34).

scene. When Mosca is interrupted by the knock of another client, he dismisses Voltore with language which raises his hopes to great heights, but is still noncommittal:

> And, gentle sir,
> When you doe come to swim, in golden lard,
> Vp to the armes, in honny, that your chin
> Is borne vp stiffe, with fatnesse of the floud,
> Thinke on your vassall; but remember me:
> I ha' not beene your worst of clients.[21]

This agility of Mosca in using ambiguities for a rhetorical purpose is highly developed. He sometimes makes statements of fact in such a way that they are disregarded or taken as mere rhetoric. Language which appears to be rhetorical to one character but which the audience recognizes as literal truth occurs in the scene in which Mosca announces Corvino's desire to offer his wife to Volpone.

Mos.	Sir, signior CORVINO, here, is come to see you.
VOLP.	Oh.
Mos.	And hearing of the consultation had, So lately, for your health, is come to offer, Or rather, sir, to prostitute—
CORV.	Thankes, sweet MOSCA.
Mos.	Freely, vn-ask'd, or vn-intreated—
CORV.	Well.
Mos.	(As the true, feruent instance of his loue) His owne most faire and proper wife; the beauty, Onely of price, in *Venice*—
CORV.	'Tis well vrg'd.[22]

Here Corvino is conscious only of Mosca's rhetorical efforts, used, as he supposes, in furthering his interests. Therefore, when Mosca changes "offer" to "prostitute," which the audience understands is more truly accurate, Corvino thanks him for using a more moving word, which he takes as a kind of hyperbole.

No emotion whatever is involved in the mountebank oration

---

[21] *Ibid.*, I, iii, 69–74 (V, 34).　　　　[22] *Ibid.*, III, vii, 72–79 (V, 79).

which Volpone makes before Celia's window. Its rhetoric is introduced primarily to complete his disguise, and it therefore follows well-worn patterns of sentence.composition:

Here is a poulder, conceal'd in this paper, of which, if I should speake to the worth, nine thousand volumes were but as one page, that page as a line, that line as a word: so short is this pilgrimage of man (which some call life) to the expressing of it. Would I reflect on the price? why, the whole world were but as an empire, that empire as a prouince, that prouince as a banke, that banke as a priuate purse, to the purchase of it. I will, onely, tell you; It is the poulder, that made VENVS *a goddesse (giuen her by* APOLLO*) that kept her perpetually yong, clear'd her wrincles, firm'd her gummes, fill'd her skin, colour'd her haire; from her, deriu'd to* HELEN, *and at the sack of* Troy *(vnfortunately) lost: till now, in this our age, it was as happily recouer'd, by a studious Antiquarie, out of some ruines of Asia, . . .*[23]

The rhetoric here is prominently displayed in anadiplosis (repeating the last word of a phrase at the beginning of the next), parathesis (speaking parenthetically), and diazeugma (using the same subject for many verbs), but it is much less productive of irony than the speeches of Mosca which have been examined. The presence of Sir Politic Wouldbe, however, gives it a dramatic interest.

The use of hyperbole by Volpone and Mosca as a means of carrying out their deception has been illustrated, and some varieties of irony which such rhetorical speech produces have been observed. A different kind of irony is produced when such speech is used by the duped characters, for, although they may use it deliberately as a means of persuasion, they are usually unaware of its real effects. When Mosca encourages Corvino to heap curses and insults on Volpone by pretending that he is deaf, the audience is impressed by the contrast between Corvino's real and pretended feelings:

CORV.   Art sure he does not heare vs?
Mos.   Sure, sir? why, looke you, credit your owne sense.

[23] *Ibid.*, II, ii, 227–41 (V, 56–57).

> The poxe approch, and adde to your diseases,
> If it would send you hence the sooner, sir.
> For, your incontinence, it hath deseru'd it
> Throughly, and throughly, and the plague to boot.
> (You may come neere, sir) would you once close
> Those filthy eyes of yours, that flow with slime,
> Like two frog-pits; and those same hanging cheeks,
> Couer'd with hide, in stead of skin: (nay, helpe, sir)
> That looke like frozen dish-clouts, set on end.

CORV.   Or, like an old smok'd wall, on which the raine
        Ran downe in streakes.

MOS.   Excellent, sir, speake out;
        You may be lowder yet: a culuering,
        Discharged in his eare, would hardly bore it.

CORV.   His nose is like a common sewre, still running.

MOS.   'Tis good! and, what his mouth?

CORV.
                                A very draught.[24]

In situations like this, the speaker is often conscious of the
hyperbole, but not of its effect. The effect of exposure is a delight to the "cony-catchers" (who are ironists with a dramatic
role) as well as to the audience. A comparable and even more
effective scene is the later one in which Corvino attempts to
persuade his wife to lie with Volpone, and thus tries with all the
art at his command to cuckold himself.

Although not especially marked by hyperbole, the rhetoric
of the speeches of Voltore before the court in defense of Volpone is among the most effective in Jonson's plays. The ironic
power of the speech is directly proportionate to its rhetorical
elaboration. The art of rhetoric is deliberately used by a character who fails to see the full effect of his speech. Voltore's
ability as a speaker is alluded to throughout the play, and,
following the great display of his eloquence before the court,
a scene between Mosca and Volpone is given to direct comment upon his language:

MOS.   Did not your Aduocate rare?

VOLP.   O (my most honor'd fathers, my graue fathers,

[24] *Ibid.*, I, v, 50–66 (V, 42–43).

Vnder correction of your father-hoods, 5,hr
What face of truth, is here? If these strange deeds
May passe, most honour'd fathers—) I had much a doe
To forbeare laughing.

. . .

Mos. He'has taken paines, in faith, sir, and deseru'd,
(In my poore iudgement, I speake it, vnder fauour,
Not to contrary you, sir) very richly—
Well—to be cosen'd.

Volp. 'Troth, and I thinke so too,
By that I heard him, in the latter end.

Mos. O, but before, sir; had you heard him, first,
Draw it to certaine heads, then aggrauate,
Then vse his vehement figures—I look'd still,
When he would shift a shirt; and, doing this
Out of pure loue, no hope of gaine—[25]

With his usual explicitness, Jonson here reviews the response of the audience to the entire court scene. In that scene, Voltone accuses Celia and Bonario with the cooperation of their husband and father respectively:

This lewd woman
(That wants no artificiall lookes, or teares,
To helpe the visor, she has now put on)
Hath long beene knowne a close adulteresse,
To that lasciuious youth there; not suspected,
I say, but knowne; and taken, in the act;
With him; and by this man, the easie husband,
Pardon'd: whose timelesse bounty makes him, now,
Stand here, the most vnhappie, innocent person,
That euer mans owne goodnesse made accus'd.[26]

The choice of words, the distribution of emphasis by careful placing of pauses, the use, among other figures, of parathesis, correction, and hyperbole, and the reasonable tone, all indicate that this is the speech of a practiced orator. The pause after "husband" (natural at the end of a line, but exaggerated with a comma) is apparently calculated to suggest that the young couple were discovered together by the husband. Jonson is fond

[25] *Ibid.*, V, ii, 32–37, 44–53 (V, 110–11). [26] *Ibid.*, IV, v, 34–43 (V, 100).

of using ambiguities which result from the line-end pause.[27]
Voltore not only takes pains, as Mosca observes, but is proud to
draw attention to the great skill of his speech and of his reason-
ing:

> (I shall here desire
> Your father-hoods to note but my collections,
> As most remarkable). . . .[28]

In the second part of his speech, when Volpone is brought on
his bed into court, Voltore mocks the charges against him as in-
credibly foolish:

> Here, here,
> The testimonie comes, that will conuince,
> And put to vtter dumbnesse their bold tongues.
> See here, graue fathers, here's the rauisher,
> The rider on mens wiues, the great impostor,
> The grand voluptuary! do you not think,
> These limbes should affect *venery?* or these eyes
> Couet a concubine? 'pray you, marke these hands.
> Are they not fit to stroake a ladies brests?
> Perhaps, he doth dissemble? [29]

Choosing his rhetorical figures with art, Voltone repeats the
charges sarcastically without suspecting how literally true they
are. He is being gulled by his own oratory, of which he is so
proud.

In *Volpone* Jonson had adapted to comedy a language of
height and gravity. *Volpone* represents the peak of his achievement with rhetorical hyperbole. Although he returned to the
familiar language of prose in *Epicoene*, it too has many rhetorical qualities. Morose's horror of noise is expressed in the play
principally by an aversion to the noise of speaking. Speech may
be reasonably described as mere noise when it is devoid of
meaning or unnecessarily wordy, and it is this kind of speech,

---

[27] Compare the example quoted above from *Poetaster*, p. 116; and Lady
Wouldbe's

> The more you see me, the more I shall conceiue,
> You haue forgot our quarrell (*Volpone*, IV, iii, 18–19).

[28] *Volpone*, IV, v, 86–88 (V, 101–102).　　[29] *Ibid.*, IV, vi, 20–29 (V, 105).

often in the form of jargon or hyperbole, that is used to torment Morose. Truewit delights in "thundring into him the incommodities of a wife, and the miseries of marriage," [30] but, as he says to Morose truly, when he visits him: "I come not to perswade you." [31] As in *Volpone* the audience is aware of the purpose of the rhetoric, and can observe its effects with detachment.

Unlike the rhetoric of *Volpone*, that of *Epicoene* expresses little or no emotion and raises no moral question. The language is marked rather by wit than emotion, real or pretended. The hyperbole of *Epicoene*, though not so prominent as in *Volpone*, is used invariably with an ironic effect. For instance, when the collegiate ladies visit Morose and are offended by Morose's manners, Truewit joins them in criticizing him: "By that light, you deserue to be grafted, and haue your hornes reach from one side of the Iland, to the other." Then, in an aside to Morose, he adds, "Doe not mistake me, sir, I but speake this, to giue the ladies some heart againe, not for any malice to you." [32] He thus continues his pretense of having Morose's welfare at heart by speaking out what he describes as a mere formula of words for its effect on the ladies. His real purpose is, of course, to increase Morose's torment. Similarly in the later scene, when Morose repents of his marriage and curses Cutbeard, who arranged the match, Truewit offers to help him invent ingenious and appropriate curses. But he is first careful to remind Morose of their uselessness:

'Tis very well, sir. If you laid on a curse or two, more, I'll assure you hee'll beare 'hem. As, that he may get the poxe with seeking to cure it, sir? Or, that while he is curling another mans haire, his owne may drop off? Or, for burning some male-baudes lock, he may haue his braine beat out with the curling-iron? [33]

His words to Morose are nothing but noise that adds to his suffering. Truewit pretends, however, to offer them as com-

[30] *Epicoene*, II, iv, 14-15 (V, 188).   [31] *Ibid.*, II, ii, 88 (V, 181).
[32] *Ibid.*, III, vi, 105-106 (V, 216).   [33] *Ibid.*, III, v, 68-73 (V, 212).

forting, and he pretends to help Morose reluctantly. Such are
the dramatic complications of the rhetoric in *Epicoene*. It is
always ironical, but its irony depends not upon the moral atti-
tudes of the audience, as frequently in *Volpone*, but upon a
simple farcical situation.

In his next play, *The Alchemist*, Jonson returns to the me-
dium of verse, and to the heightened language of *Volpone*. Like
Volpone and Mosca, Subtle and Face in *The Alchemist* use rhet-
oric to persuade their dupes to gull themselves. In order to put
Dapper off from the promised visit of his "aunt of *Faerie*,"
Face instructs him:

> Sir, against one a clock, prepare your selfe.
> Till when you must be fasting; onely, take
> Three drops of vinegar, in, at your nose;
> Two at your mouth; and one, at either eare;
> Then, bath your fingers endes; and wash your eyes;
> To sharpen your fiue senses; and, cry *hum*,
> Thrise; and then *buz*, as often; and then, come.[34]

Face here deliberately exaggerates his instructions to an ab-
surdity which exposes Dapper's blindness, and makes him responsible for his own gulling. Although this language is understood literally by Dapper, and not as an exaggerated manner of
speaking, it creates for the audience an effect of irony not unlike
that which Jonson got from hyperbole used in rhetorical persuasion.

Hyperbole is used with ironic effect by the gulled characters
in *The Alchemist*, as it had been in *Volpone*. One of these, Sir
Epicure Mammon, is like Volpone himself a "grand volup-
tuary." A comparison between the scenes of love-making in the
two plays is enlightening. Unlike Volpone, Mammon uses
hyperbole and other devices of rhetoric quite unaware of their
effect. When he makes love to Doll Common, like Volpone addressing Celia, he uses hyperbole for two purposes, first, to express his own deep emotion, and, secondly, to persuade her. But,

[34] *The Alchemist*, I, ii, 164–70 (V, 308).

unlike Volpone, he rarely sees himself in a dramatic light, and, instead of using language with mastery, he is victimized by it. The audience is also more carefully prepared to listen to Mammon's love-making with full consciousness of its rhetorical purpose:

> Now, Epicvre,
> Heighten thy selfe, talke to her, all in gold;
> Raine her as many showers, as Iove did drops
> Vnto his Danae: Shew the *God* a miser,
> Compar'd with Mammon. What? the *stone* will do't.
> Shee shall feele gold, tast gold, heare gold, sleepe gold:
> Nay, we will *concumbere* gold. I will be puissant,
> And mightie in my talke to her! [35]

Volpone's language is not so pointed to. When Mammon makes love it is clear that he is gulling himself. Instead of addressing a virtuous Celia, he addresses the cheats' prostitute, Doll Common, whose purpose it is to encourage her would-be lover. His making love, which he does with such painstaking art, finally justifies Subtle's failure to produce the philosopher's stone. Doll's encouragement is crafty. She pretends to be coy and protests against Mammon's persuasion; it is thus brought once more to the attention of the audience:

> This art, sir, i'your words,
> Calls your whole faith in question.[36]

But Mammon is so moved that he is scarcely conscious of using hyperbole at all. He announces with full conviction that she is now "lady" of the philosopher's stone:

> Thinke therefore, thy first wish, now; let me heare it:
> And it shall raine into thy lap, no shower,
> But flouds of gold, whole cataracts, a deluge,
> To get a nation on thee! [37]

Such hyperbole has an effect quite unlike that of *Tamburlaine*. Tamburlaine may have spoken "in the same terms" [38] as Mam-

[35] *Ibid.*, IV, i, 24–31 (V, 360).   [36] *Ibid.*, IV, i, 71–72 (V, 361).
[37] *Ibid.*, IV, i, 125–28 (V, 363).   [38] Gregory Smith, *Ben Jonson*, p. 115.

mon, but Jonson has succeeded in giving the language a new dramatic value.

It is not without significance that *Volpone* followed one of Jonson's tragedies, and that *The Alchemist* was followed by the other. In no other comedies is Jonson's language more elevated and more essentially formal than in these two. In this respect their language approaches the language of tragedy, as Jonson understood it. *Catiline* is a rhetorical tragedy; its language is declamatory and its dramatic progress depends upon oratory. That rhetoric is the basis for the growth of the plot is made explicit by one of the choruses, when it comments on the action:

> What age is this, where honest men,
>   Plac'd at the helme,
> A sea of some foule mouth, or pen,
>   Shall ouer-whelme?
> And call their diligence, deceipt;
>   Their vertue, vice;
> Their watchfulnesse, but lying in wait;
>   And bloud, the price.
> O, let vs plucke this euill seede
>   Out of our spirits;
> And giue, to euery noble deede,
>   The name it merits.[39]

Catiline's conspiracy is organized and forwarded by the abuse of the art of speaking, here described by the chorus, and the conspiracy is finally overthrown by Cicero's oratory. The central scene of the play is Cicero's long oration against Catiline which is doubtless longer than its dramatic interest would allow, but Jonson was interested in historical accuracy as well as dramatic necessity. In answering the charge, Catiline uses the stock argument against oratory:

> If an oration, or high language, *Fathers*,
> Could make me guiltie, here is one, hath done it:
> H'has stroue to emulate this mornings thunder,
> With his prodigious rhetoricke. But I hope,

[39] *Catiline*, IV, 879–90 (V, 526).

> This *Senate* is more graue, then to giue credit
> Rashly to all he vomits, 'gainst a man
> Of your owne order, a *Patrician;*
> And one, whose ancestors haue more deseru'd
> Of *Rome*, then this mans eloquence could vtter,
> Turn'd the best way: as still, it is the worst.[40]

Each phrase is chosen for its value in persuasion, and a moment later Catiline introduces the derogatory epithet for Cicero which he had already made famous in Rome, "a poore petty inmate." [41]

Most hyperbole in *Catiline* expresses genuine feeling worthy of respect. The leading characters maintain their dignity more consistently than in *Sejanus*. Public oratory, which fills many lines of the play, has a rhetorical purpose, but is not ironical. When Catiline, for example, urges his fellow conspirators to "break the yron yoke, forg'd for our necks," and asks them, "What lesse can we call it?" [42] his rhetoric is used in simple persuasion. Hyperbole is used also in the dialogue to express strong personal feelings. When the conspiracy is threatening, Cato says:

> Though heauen should speake, with all his wrath at once,
> That, with his breath, the hinges of the world
> Did cracke, we should stand vpright, and vnfear'd.[43]

Cethegus, "a spirit of right MARTIAN breed," also finds hyperbole a natural form of expression. He is always impatient to act:

> This time
> Had beene enough, t'haue scatter'd all the starres,
> T'haue quench'd the sunne, and moone, and made the world
> Despaire of day, or any light, but ours.[44]

This hyperbole resembles that of Envy's Prologue in *Poetaster;* it is to be accepted by the audience as an expression of feeling, although not on a strictly human level. The character

[40] *Ibid.*, IV, 462–71 (V, 512).
[41] *Ibid.*, IV, 479 (V, 513); cf. II, 115–16 (V, 458).
[42] *Ibid.*, I, 345–46 (V, 446).   [43] *Ibid.*, IV, 30–32 (V, 499).
[44] *Ibid.*, IV, 758–61 (V, 522).

is idealized and heightened, and the language which it speaks is a stylization of natural speech.

But the use of the art of rhetoric for dramatic irony is not entirely absent from *Catiline*. The conspiracy is really defeated by Fulvia who had been entrusted with Catiline's secret by her lover Curius. There are sharp contrasts between the speech of Cicero and that of Fulvia which are used to suggest the great difference between their characters. When Cicero is first informed of the conspiracy he reflects upon it, and is joined by Fulvia:

> CIC. And, then, to take a horride sacrament
>   In humane bloud, for execution
>   Of this their dire designe; which might be call'd
>   The height of wickednesse: but that, that was higher,
>   For which they did it!
> FVL.   I assure your lordship,
>   The extreme horror of it almost turn'd me
>   To aire, when first I heard it; I was all
>   A vapor, when 'twas told me: and I long'd
>   To vent it any where. 'Twas such a secret,
>   I thought, it would haue burnt me vp.[45]

The obvious contrast here is between a diction strong and full-sounding, and one which is weak and flat; and secondly, between a finely controlled rhythm and one which is marked by nervous, stuttering pauses. The contrast is important because it emphasizes the irony involved in the character and motives of Fulvia. Cicero himself remarks on the strangeness of Rome's being saved by "a base and common strumpet." Fulvia explains to Curius her motive in betraying the conspirators:

> Come, doe you thinke, I'ld walke in any plot,
> Where madame SEMPRONIA should take place of me,
> And FVLVIA come i'the *rere*, or o'the *by?*
> That I would be her second. . . .[46]

[45] *Ibid.*, III, 283–92 (V, 478).   [46] *Ibid.*, III, 375–78 (V, 481).

This is the irony of Jonsonian comedy, but, as Herford and Simpson observe,[47] it does not seem out of keeping with the tone of Jonson's tragedy. The comic element is part of the main action itself, not anything like mere comic relief. The contrast between the characters of Cicero and Fulvia is again emphasized when together they try to persuade Curius to betray the conspirators. Cicero the accomplished speaker is sententious, and he chooses epithets which are emotionally persuasive.

> Bad men excuse their faults, good men will leaue 'hem.
> He acts the third crime, that defends the first.
>
> . . .
>
> . . . be not afraid, to breake
> With murderers, and traytors, for the sauing
> A life, so neere, and necessary to you,
> As is your countries. Thinke but on her right.
> No child can be too naturall to his parent.[48]

Fulvia, on the other hand, before Curius answers, says ingenuously, "his shame, yet, stayes him," thus reminding him of what Cicero tried to make him forget. Her argument to Curius is simple: "Apply Your selfe to me, and the *Consul*, and be wise." When Cicero discovers what she has said, he immediately improves upon her phrase by exaggerating it:

> FVL.   Sir, you may heare. I tell him, in the way,
>   Wherein he was, how hazardous his course was.
> CIC.   How hazardous? how certayne to all ruine.[49]

The division of Fulvia's lines with the awkward pause after "way" is part of the ignoble vulgarity which makes her argue only from the "hazard" which Curius runs in supporting Catiline. Here, as in Jonson's comedies, the art of speaking marks an ironic contrast.

In *Bartholomew Fair*, Jonson returns to prose and to a language nearer that of *Epicoene* than that of *Volpone* and *The*

---

[47] *Ben Jonson*, II, 126–27.   [48] *Catiline*, III, 339–40, 361–65 (V, 480).
[49] *Ibid.*, III, 385–87 (V, 481).

Alchemist. Rhetorical speech is frequently the polished speech of a witty character. When Quarlous attacks his friend Winwife as a widow-hunter, his formal invective is marked by hyperbole:

A sweet course for a man to waste the brand of life for, to be still raking himselfe a fortune in an old womans embers; we shall ha' thee, after thou hast beene but a moneth marryed to one of 'hem, looke like the *quartane ague*, and the black *Iaundise* met in a face, and walke as if thou had'st borrow'd legges of a *Spinner*, and voyce of a *Cricket*.[50]

This is the kind of wit that Dryden wanted more of in Jonson. Such an encounter between two witty gentlemen, however, could not produce the irony that is characteristic of *Volpone*. The wit of the speech is practically independent of a dramatic context, and gains very little from it. The wit of Winwife and Quarlous, when they invent epithets for Ursula the pig woman, is equally independent, and so is the wit of Wasp when he says to his charge Cokes:

. . . he that had the meanes to trauell your head, now, should meet finer sights then any are i' the *Fayre;* and make a finer voyage on't; to see it all hung with cockleshels, pebbles, fine wheat-strawes, and here and there, a chicken's feather, and a cob-web. . . .[51]

These speeches recall the ironic character descriptions of Jonson's Humor comedies. The irony of *Bartholomew Fair* is nearer to that of those plays than to the irony of *Volpone*. It is more often expressed directly through characters like Wasp than through a dramatic action. Persuasive speech is less important than characteristic speech.

The two characters in this play whose speech is made most conspicuous by their exaggerated use of rhetorical devices are Justice Overdo and Zeal Busy. Overdo's speech is pompous, oratorical, and affected. It is full of classical allusions and such obvious rhetorical figures as paradigma (example), correction

[50] *Bartholomew Fair*, I, iii, 77–83 (VI, 25).
[51] *Ibid.*, I, v, 93–97 (VI, 33–34).

("what doe we know? nay, what can wee know?" [52]), hy-
pophora (asking a question and answering it oneself), epizeuxis
("thirst not after it, youth: thirst not after it" [53]), auxesis ("hath
not a Snaile, a Spider, yea, a Neuft bin found there" [54]), parathesis, and apostrophe. He refers to his speeches as "orations" [55] and compliments himself on a "pretty gradation." [56]
The simple Bartholomew Cokes is impressed by his "braue
words" [57] and "a fine similitude" [58] which he uses. These explicit comments on his rhetoric help to keep alive the interest of
the audience in it. What is most characteristic, as his name suggests, is that he overdoes the use of all figures. Not content with
one example, he uses six:

I had thought once, at one speciall blow he ga' me, to haue reueal'd
my selfe; but then (I thank thee, fortitude) I remembred that a
wise man (and who is euer so great a part o' the Common-wealth
in himselfe) for no particular disaster ought to abandon a publike
good designe. The husbandman ought not for one vnthankful
yeer, to forsake the plough; The Shepheard ought not, for one
scabb'd sheep, to throw by his tar-boxe; The Pilot ought not for
one leake i' the poope, to quit the Helme; Nor the Alderman
ought not for one custerd more, at a meale, to giue vp his cloake;
The Constable ought not to breake his staffe, and forsweare the
watch, for one roaring night; Nor the Piper o' the Parish (*Vt
paruis componere magna solebam*) to put vp his pipes, for one
rainy Sunday.[59]

This exaggeration is parallel to the exaggerated use of jargon
and hyperbole in *Volpone* and *The Alchemist*, but its irony is
closer to that of the early Humor comedies. It is not due to a
dramatic situation, but merely to a display of character by
which the audience, as a critical spectator, can see the difference
between Overdo's conception of himself and what he really is.

The language of Zeal Busy is ironic in a similar way. His
speech is also pompous, oratorical, and affected; the parallel be-

[52] *Ibid.*, II, i, 28–29 (VI, 40).   [53] *Ibid.*, II, vi, 14 (VI, 56).
[54] *Ibid.*, II, vi, 13–14 (VI, 56).   [55] *Ibid.*, III, iii, 1 (VI, 66).
[56] *Ibid.*, III, iii, 19–20 (VI, 66). [57] *Ibid.*, II, vi, 23 (VI, 56).
[58] *Ibid.*, II, vi, 45 (VI, 57).   [59] *Ibid.*, III, iii, 21–34 (VI, 66–67).

tween the two characters, as representative of two branches of authority, seems to be part of Jonson's intention. Busy also uses to excess some of the more obvious rhetorical figures. Epizeuxis is a favorite with him as well as Overdo (". . . it were a sinne of obstinacy, great obstinacy, high and horrible obstinacy, to decline, or resist . . ." [60]); other figures which mark the quality of his speech clearly are isocolon (". . . let not your eyes be drawne aside with vanity, nor your eare with noyses" [61]), systrophe ("the place is *Smithfield*, or the field of Smiths . . . the wares are the wares of diuels" [62]), paraphrasis (". . . satisfie your wiues frailty. Let your fraile wife be satisfied" [63]). Like Overdo, Busy uses figures without a sense of decorum, and the effect of his speech is due to the exaggerated use of them:

I wil remoue *Dagon* there, I say, that *Idoll*, that heathenish *Idoll*, that remaines (as I may say) a beame, a very beame, not a beame of the *Sunne*, nor a beame of the *Moone*, nor a beame of a ballance, neither a house-beame, nor a Weauers beame, but a beame in the eye, in the eye of the brethren; a very great beame, an exceeding great beame. . . .[64]

This language is not so undramatic that it is to be taken merely as a satire on the speech of Puritans; its dramatic value is in the light it casts on the character of Zeal Busy. It is ironic because the audience is always able to recognize the difference beween what the language pretends to be, and what it really is. It is not the effect of the language on other characters that is primarily important, nor the peculiar situation in which the speaker is seen. The conception of such a character is itself ironical, and it is conveyed to the theater audience primarily through the representation of speech.

In Jonson's next play the decline of his dramatic power begins to show itself. Though the hyperbole is strikingly Jonsonian in the following lines from *The Devil Is an Ass*, it lacks the irony

[60] *Ibid.*, III, ii, 81-82 (VI, 64).   [61] *Ibid.*, III, ii, 31-32 (VI, 62).
[62] *Ibid.*, III, ii, 39-41 (VI, 63).   [63] *Ibid.*, III, ii, 85-86 (VI, 64).
[64] *Ibid.*, V, v, 4-10 (VI, 133).

that is characteristic of such language in Jonson's greatest comedies:

> O! I could shoote mine eyes at him, for that, now;
> Or leaue my teeth in'him, were they cuckolds bane,
> Inough to kill him. What prodigious,
> Blinde, and most wicked change of fortune's this?
> I ha' no ayre of patience: all my vaines
> Swell, and my sinewes start at iniquity of it.
> I shall breake, breake.[65]

These lines are provoked by Fitzdottrel's treatment of his wife. Wittipol, the speaker, is an intelligent gentleman sympathetically represented. No irony arises from the language in relation either to his character or to the dramatic situation. Hyperbole is a mere convention of expression, not so appropriate to his character as it was to that of, say, Macilente in *Every Man Out of His Humor*. Though this passage is not representative of the best verse in *The Devil Is an Ass*, it represents the quality of hyperbole in Jonson's last comedies. In *The New Inn* and *The Magnetic Lady*, in which hyperbole is not uncommon, it is even more grotesque than in the passage just quoted. The rhetorical qualities of Jonson's language remain, but they have little dramatic interest. In *The New Inn*, when the Court of Love is dissolved, Lovel is deeply moved:

> O my braine!
> How art thou turned! and my blood congeald!
> My sinewes slackned! and my marrow melted!
> That I remember not where I haue bin,
> Or what I am? Only my tongue's on fire;
> And burning downward, hurles forth coales, & cinders,
> To tell, this temple of loue, will soone be ashes!
>   . . .
> I will goe catch the wind first in a sieue,
> Weigh smoak, and measure shadowes, plough the water,
> And sow my hopes there, ere I stay in *Loue*.[66]

[65] *The Devil Is an Ass*, II, vii, 17–23 (VI, 205).
[66] *The New Inn*, IV, iv, 257–63, 269–71 (VI, 476).

Lady Frampul uses language of a similar quality to express her devotion to Lovel:

> Thou doest not know my suffrings, what I feele,
> My fires, and feares, are met: I burne, and freeze,
> My liuer's one great coale, my heart shrunke vp
> With all the fiuers, and the masse of blood
> Within me, is a standing lake of fire,
> Curl'd with the cold wind of my gelid sighs,
> That driue a drift of sleete through all my body,
> And shoot a *February* through my veines.
> Vntil I see him, I am drunke with thirst,
> And surfeted with hunger of his presence.[67]

This is Jonsonian hyperbole gone to seed. It has the extravagance of the language of *Volpone* without its irony. The audience is expected to accept this language as an expression of strong, natural feeling.

The language of Jonson's pastoral play, *The Sad Shepherd*, is not marked especially by hyperbole, and when it appears, it lacks the ironic effect most characteristic of its use in Jonson's other plays. It is not unlike the hyperbole in the speech of Jonson's unreal characters like Envy's Prologue in *Poetaster*, or Sylla's ghost in *Catiline*. It also resembles the hyperbole which sometimes appears in Jonson's masques. The witches' Dame in *The Masque of Queens*, for instance, describes as follows the season in which she rides forth:

> You, that haue seene me ride, When *Hecate*
> Durst not take chariot; When the boystrous Sea,
> Wᵗhout a breath of Wind, hath knocked the skie;
> And that hath thundred, *Ioue* not knowing, Why:
> When we haue set the Elements at warres;
> Made Mid-night see the Sunne; and Day the starres. . . .[68]

The speaker here is supposedly not exaggerating, and in her unreal world the language can be considered as natural. The same is true of the speech of Maudlin in *The Sad Shepherd*. The

[67] *The New Inn*, V, ii, 45–54 (VI, 481).
[68] *The Masque of Queens*, ll. 224–29 (VII, 295).

exaggeration is a convention of speaking, but it does not have the effect of exaggeration in *The Spanish Tragedy* or in *Tamburlaine* because the characters who use it are so unreal; it is never treated as an expression of natural emotion.

The use of hyperbole which distinguishes Jonson, however, and which has been described in this and the preceding chapter, is that which produces or enhances comic irony. Exaggeration is a characteristic of Jonson's style. The development of his use of jargon illustrates the growth of a conscious purpose in exaggeration. Partly through exaggeration, rhetoric is impressed upon the consciousness of the audience to produce a dramatic effect. The rhetorical figure which by definition is an exaggerated way of speaking is hyperbole, and the figure of hyperbole seems particularly suited to Jonson's dramatic purposes. It is a prominent mark of his language. He found it useful because its rhetorical aim is obvious. If it is used, as Jonson sometimes uses it, to express an emotion with which the audience cannot sympathize, it draws further attention to itself. It is also often used in Jonson's plays in persuasion, and, since the audience is then aware of the rhetorical aim of the speaker, it is made aware of the art which he applies. Comments of various characters also point out the rhetorical quality of a speech. In *Volpone* and *The Alchemist*, Jonson's gravest and most elevated comedies, hyperbole becomes an important part of the technique of comic irony.

CHAPTER VIII

CONCLUSION

IT HAS NOT been the aim of this study to describe what Hardin Craig calls Jonson's "perfection as a rhetorician." [1] A study confined to the application of rhetorical principles of composition would be concerned only with what Socrates called the "preliminaries" of drama. It might attempt to classify the tropes and figures of Jonson's language, and would include a study of the structure of his sentences. The composition of dramatic speeches would be analyzed, and compared with that taught by the rhetoricians. But such a study would not necessarily prove the writer's acquaintance with rhetoric as an art, nor would it necessarily be relevant to criticism. In the first place, as J. M. Manly points out, [2] some tropes and figures have always been used to express human feeling. Furthermore, since the rhetorical divisions of a sentence or a speech are only based upon reason and the best practice, it would be difficult to determine what in fact is due to the study of rhetoric, what to reason and the observation of the best practice. A writer who profits by the study of rhetoric does not have its precepts stored in compartments of his mind. They are so assimilated as to inform his own native judgment.

Despite these difficulties, the debt of certain writers to the study of rhetoric is of course clear, and not impossible to investigate. If the rhetorical characteristics of their work seem particularly artificial, they have probably applied certain principles of rhetoric self-consciously. One feels reasonably certain about the influence in *The Spanish Tragedy* or *Locrine*. If the technical vocabulary of rhetoric is prominent, that too is per-

[1] *The Enchanted Glass* (New York, 1936), p. 169.
[2] "Chaucer and the Rhetoricians," *Proceedings of the British Academy*, 1926, pp. 14–15.

haps an indication of the writer's consciousness of rhetorical principles. The vocabulary is very noticeable in Marston and Chapman as well as Jonson. In some Elizabethan books the application of the principles of rhetoric is made quite clear by notes in the margin which name the figure being used. In Sidney's *Arcadia* the rhetoric of a speech is sometimes commented upon by another speaker. In the drama one is made aware of the author's consciousness of rhetoric when the rhetorical quality of a speech in the dialogue is commented upon by another character, or by the speaker himself. References to the art of certain speakers are especially prominent in Ben Jonson. This fact suggests at once the possible importance of rhetoric in his plays, and some criterion for judging its presence. The study of Jonson's rhetoric has here been limited to the rhetoric of which the audience is made aware, either by an explicit comment, like the discussion of Voltore's speech in defense of Volpone, or by the tone, as in the opening soliloquy of Volpone. This awareness gives the rhetorical quality in the dialogue of Jonson's plays dramatic significance. The final emphasis of the study of such rhetoric is on dramatic effect, but the study of tropes, sentences, and speeches is not irrelevant. These details, like the quality of rhetoric itself, have a dramatic meaning, and their study may be enlightening for the critic as well as the student of rhetoric. Those speeches which are explicitly or implicitly treated by Jonson as rhetorical are not isolated or difficult to discover. The chronological surveys of the foregoing chapters have shown how pervasive they are. They are most conspicuous in the plays which are widely regarded as Jonson's greatest, *Volpone* and *The Alchemist*, and the particular speeches which are commonly pointed to as typically Jonsonian are characterized by this rhetorical quality.

In order to examine the uses of such rhetoric in Jonson, two rhetorical characteristics of his diction were chosen for special study. The dramatic effects of jargon and hyperbole are perhaps representative of the effects of other rhetorical elements in the plays. Whether the language is used, as in the earlier comedies, to exhibit human folly by representing a foolish character through his speech, or whether, as in the mature plays, it is used in a dramatic action, often as persuasive rhetoric which makes folly expose itself, its effect is always to enhance the spectator's sense of irony. In the earlier plays, the language forces the audience into an attitude of watchful detachment. In the later, such as *Volpone* and *The Alchemist*, the language also constantly plays upon the dramatic situation and enriches its meaning. It is this kind of richness, quite different from Shakespeare's, that is Ben Jonson's distinction.

Shakespeare's irony in comedy is different from Jonson's, and its effect depends less upon the use of language as such. It is Jonson's constant practice to make his audience conscious of the language which his characters use. Shakespeare, on the other hand, generally makes his audience attend upon what is said, not the way it is said.[3] Exceptions may be noted. There are instances when Shakespeare, like Jonson and other Elizabethans, makes his comic characters reveal their folly through the quality of their speech. The blunders of Andrew Aguecheek produce the simple kind of irony which is common in Jonson's earlier plays. It depends upon the position of conscious superiority in which the audience is placed. But Shakespeare never greatly refined his satiric comedy,[4] as Jonson did, and this kind of irony which is dependent upon language is not characteristic of his style. His language is perhaps more subtly appropriate to his characters than Jonson's, but it is not so often a source of comic irony.

The irony of Shakespeare's comedy is often directly expressed in the speeches of his witty characters, including many of those who are called fools. Prince Hal and Falstaff self-

[3] Compare Upton's remark on Jonson's borrowing: "Jonson is always desirous that his imitations should appear; Shakespeare lies more concealed" (*Remarks on Three Plays of Benjamin Jonson*, London, 1749, p. 88).

[4] E. E. Stoll, *Shakespeare Studies* (New York, 1927), p. 181.

consciously affect Puritan phrases and sentence patterns,[5] and they themselves have a sense of irony. The irony is not dramatic, except in so far as it suits the character of the person using it. When Jonson's Subtle affects Puritan terms in addressing Mammon, he is also somewhat of an ironist, but the speech is dramatic in a wider sense, because it has a function in a dramatic action. The irony of Subtle's speech is more dependent upon the situation than that of Falstaff's. Although Subtle is an ironist, he is also an impostor, and the audience listens to him with ironic detachment, while it moves in sympathy with Falstaff. Touchstone is equally self-conscious in using polished forms of oratory. When Audrey accepts his marriage proposal, he says:

Amen. A man may, if he were of a fearful heart, stagger in this attempt; for here we have no temple but the wood, no assembly but horn-beasts. But what though? Courage! As horns are odious, they are necessary. It is said, "Many a man knows no end of his goods." Right! Many a man has good horns and knows no end of them. Well, that is the dowry of his wife; 'tis none of his own getting. Horns? Even so. Poor men alone? No, no! the noblest deer hath them as huge as the rascal. Is the single man therefore blessed? No; as a wall'd town is more worthier than a village, so is the forehead of a married man more honourable than the bare brow of a bachelor; and by how much defence is better than no skill, by so much is a horn more precious than to want.[6]

This speech may be compared to Falstaff's speech on honor. Both Falstaff and Touchstone see themselves with ironic detachment, and in dispraising honor or in praising the horn, they use forms of speech familiar in oratory. Their oratorical style is not used in order to persuade or deceive some other character, but only to set the ironic tone of their reflections. Jonson's characters often see themselves in a dramatic light and affect artful speech for purposes of persuasion, but such direct comic irony as this is unknown in his plays. In his opening soliloquy Volpone, like Touchstone, praises in high style what is not consid-

[5] *Henry IV*, Part I, I, ii, 81–82, 91–99. [6] *As You Like It*, III, iii, 48–64.

ered by the audience praiseworthy, but his speech is ironic only to the audience, not to Volpone. The critics among Jonson's characters, like Surly, do not have an ironic view which includes themselves, and they lack Falstaff's and Touchstone's sense of humor. A closer analogy to this kind of comic irony in Shakespeare is found in some speeches of Chapman's comedies; they are similarly constructed on rhetorical principles, and their comic effect is partly due to their rhetorical quality.

Such is the long oration in praise of the cuckold's horn at the end of *All Fools*. Like that of Falstaff or Touchstone, its irony is the direct expression of the speaker, but unlike Falstaff or Touchstone, the speaker has come completely out of his dramatic role, as if to speak an epilogue. Comparable speeches had appeared earlier in *The Gentleman Usher;* but Poggio's speech in praise of a broom, and Fungus's in praise of a rush are slightly more dramatic because they represent a rhetorical display which exposes the folly of these characters. Like Erasmus in *The Praise of Folly*, Fungus mentions Homer's battle between the frogs and the mice as a precedent for his speech. The tradition which the mock encomium of Erasmus represents was used by other Elizabethan dramatists than Jonson. In Chapman and in Marston, the form is conspicuous and sometimes is quite undramatic, serving little purpose in the dialogue and not appropriate to the character speaking it. In Shakespeare, the character who uses such language does so with perfect appropriateness, and with rich comic effect, but the language is not active in forwarding the dramatic action or in heightening the irony of a dramatic situation. Jonson alone has translated the satirical encomium into purely dramatic terms, and made its effect depend not only upon the direct irony of a set speech, spoken in or out of character, but also upon the irony which arises from a dramatic situation.

The comic irony in Shakespeare which is dependent upon a situation is usually produced by the artificial stage convention of disguise, or mistaken identity. Viola's disguise in *Twelfth*

Night produces many situations of ironic interest to the audience, but their effect is artificial. In Jonson the ironic self-deception or the exhibition of folly has a more substantial meaning because it involves character, and casts a light upon the real world. Jonson like Shakespeare uses disguise, but it is often a disguise of speech which would be apparent to any free intelligence. The language of Mosca, Subtle, and Face is made obviously rhetorical to the audience; its falseness would be obvious to their dupes if they were not blinded by avarice, or pride, or ambition. But Shakespeare's audience can hardly blame Orlando for not recognizing Rosalind when she is disguised as Ganymede. As Ganymede she pretends to be Rosalind, and makes a dupe of Orlando, so that she may at the same time indulge her own love, and preserve her modesty. The irony which results is perhaps typical of Shakespearean comedy. The audiences sympathizes with the motives of both characters, and is able to see, with a superior ironic view of the situation, how near and yet how far Orlando is from the truth. Sentimental irony of this kind is unknown in Jonson. A situation which is similar in some ways is that between Doll Common and Mammon. As in *As You Like It*, the irony is due to the knowledge of the audience and the ignorance of one of the lovers. But the irony of the scene in *The Alchemist* gains its force not only from the immediate situation, but from the entire action which has led up to it. Irony in Jonson is more pervasive than in Shakespeare. It is not limited to isolated scenes or dependent merely upon a conventional disguise. It arises from an ironic view of life in which vice and folly among men seem constantly to expose themselves. The stage convention of disguise, therefore, seems unimportant.

The great learning which appears in Jonson's plays is sometimes felt to interfere with the purposes of comedy, and to represent his pedantry, or merely his conscientious attempt to be realistic and accurate. Much of his learning, however, is contained in consciously written rhetorical speeches, which are understood by the audience to have a rhetorical purpose. These speeches are dramatic, and the learning is directed toward the achievement of dramatic effects. The abundance, even the excess, of learned terms or allusions is often Jonson's considered artistic intention. The development of his style is marked by an increasingly bold use of professional jargons, and the very figure of exaggeration itself is used to excess by ordinary standards of judgment. But the effects at which Jonson aimed are dependent upon the awareness of language in the audience. Jonsonian exaggeration helps to create this awareness, and at the same time produces or enhances dramatic irony./

The evidence collected in this study will perhaps show that as long as Jonson was capable of creating situations the irony of which could only be increased by the excess of rhetoric, the method was successful. In the period of his maturity, there was no monotony in his application of the method. But in his last plays, when the quality of the language no longer forms a consistent commentary on the characters and action, the method fails. Dramatic irony is no longer produced in direct proportion to the rhetorical exaggeration of the language.

The connection between Jonson's language and his irony suggests the proper relation between his realism and the rhetorical language which seems so characteristic of his style. Some kinds of rhetoric are perhaps incompatible with realism, but the rhetorical speech which is characteristic of Jonson is the language of life as Jonson sees it. It is the language of lies and pretenses. "Wee take pleasure in the lye, and are glad, wee can cousen our selves," Jonson wrote.[7] Like Bacon and other students of rhetoric, he recognized the capacity of words not only to express genuine feeling and thought, but to deceive and to misguide. A person who sees humanity as divided primarily between knaves and fools would see the language of men most commonly used as a means of pretense and deception. The art

---

[7] *Discoveries*, in *Ben Jonson*, ed. C. H. Herford, Percy and Evelyn Simpson (10 vols., Oxford, 1925–), VIII, 607.

by which such language may be made effective is the art of rhetoric. Rhetoric is therefore the most suitable expression for Jonsonian realism. Jonson was always a dramatist and a poet, never merely a rhetorician. The richness and variety of dramatic effects which he created with rhetoric are revealed by a study of his language.

BIBLIOGRAPHY OF
WORKS CITED

Adams, Joseph Quincy. "The Sources of Ben Jonson's *Volpone*." *Modern Philology*, II (1904–5), 289–99.

Ameringer, Thomas E. The Stylistic Influence of the Second Sophistic on the Panegyrical Sermons of St. John Chrysostom. Washington, 1932.

Aristotle. The Poetics. With an English translation by W. H. Fyfe. London and New York, 1927. Loeb Classical Library.

—— The "Art" of Rhetoric. With an English translation by John Henry Freese. London and New York, 1926. Loeb Classical Library.

Ascham, Roger. The Scholemaster. In *English Works*, edited by William A. Wright. Cambridge, England, 1904.

Atkins, John William Hay. Literary Criticism in Antiquity. 2 vols. Cambridge, England, 1934.

Augustine, St. De Doctrina Christiana. Translated by J. F. Shaw. In *The Works of Aurelius Augustine, Bishop of Hippo*, edited by Marcus Dods (3d ed., 15 vols., Edinburgh, 1883), Vol. IX.

Bacon, Francis. Of the Advancement of Learning. In *The Works*, edited by James Spedding, Robert Leslie Ellis, and Douglas Denon Heath (15 vols., Boston, 1860–64), Vol. VI.

Baldwin, Charles Sears. Medieval Rhetoric and Poetic. New York, 1928.

—— Renaissance Literary Theory and Practice. New York, 1939.

Baldwin, Edward Chauncey. "Ben Jonson's Indebtedness to the Greek Character-sketch." *Modern Language Notes*, XVI (1901), 193–98.

Baskervill, Charles Read. English Elements in Jonson's Early Comedy. Austin, 1911. "University of Texas Studies in English," I.

Berdan, John M. Early Tudor Poetry 1485–1547. New York, 1920.

Boas, Frederick S. University Drama in the Tudor Age. Oxford, 1914.

Boissier, Gaston. La Fin du Paganisme. 2d ed., 2 vols. Paris, 1894.

Bradbrook, Muriel Clara. Themes and Conventions of Elizabethan Tragedy. Cambridge, England, 1935.

Bradley, Jesse F., and Joseph Quincy Adams. The Jonson Allusion-Book. New Haven, 1922.

Brinsley, John. Ludus Literarius; or, The Grammar Schoole. Edited by E. T. Campagnac. Liverpool and London, 1917.

Burton, Robert. The Anatomy of Melancholy. Edited by Floyd Dell and Paul Jordan-Smith. New York [1927].

Campbell, James M. The Influence of the Second Sophistic on the Style of the Sermons of St. Basil the Great. Washington, 1922.

Campbell, Oscar James. Comicall Satyre and Shakespeare's Troilus and Cressida. San Marino, Calif., 1938.

Carpenter, Frederic I. Metaphor and Simile in the Minor Elizabethan Drama. Chicago, 1895.

Castiglione, Baldassare. The Book of the Courtier. Translated by Sir Thomas Hoby. London, 1900. The Tudor Translations.

Chambers, Sir Edmund K. The Mediaeval Stage. 2 vols. Oxford, 1903.

Chapman, George. The Plays and Poems of George Chapman: the Comedies. Edited by Thomas Marc Parrott. London, 1914.

Chaucer, Geoffrey. Complete Works. Edited by Fred Norris Robinson. Boston, 1933.

Cheke, Sir John. "Letter to Sir Thomas Hoby." In Castiglione, *The Book of the Courtier* (Tudor Translations, London, 1900).

Cicero. De oratore. With an English translation by E. W. Sutton and H. Rackham. 2 vols. Cambridge, Mass. and London, 1942. Loeb Classical Library.

Cleland, James. The Institution of a Young Nobleman. Oxford, 1607.

Coleridge, Samuel Taylor. Miscellaneous Criticism. Edited by Thomas Middleton Raysor. London, 1936.

Cooper, Lane. An Aristotelian Theory of Comedy, with an Adaptation of the Poetics and a Translation of the 'Tractatus Coislinianus.' New York, 1922.

Coote, Edmund. The English Schoole-Master. London, 1596.

Cornford, Francis M. The Origin of Attic Comedy. London, 1914.

Craig, Hardin. The Enchanted Glass. New York, 1936.

Day, Angel. The English Secretorie: Also a Declaration of All Tropes and Figures. London, 1586.

Dibdin, Charles. A Complete History of the English Stage. 5 vols. London, 1800.

Dryden, John. "Preface" to *An Evening's Love.* In *The Dramatic*

Works, edited by Montagu Summers (6 vols., London, 1931), Vol. II.

Eliot, Thomas Stearns. Selected Essays. London, 1932.

Elyot, Sir Thomas. The Governour. London and New York, 1907. Everyman's Library.

Erasmus, Desiderius. The Praise of Folly. Edited by Mrs. P. S. Allen. Oxford, 1913.

Faral, Edmond. Les Arts poétiques du xiie et du xiiie siècle. Paris, 1924.

Fielding, Henry. Joseph Andrews, edited by George Saintsbury (2 vols., London, 1893), Preface.

Fortescue, John William. "Hunting." In *Shakespeare's England* (2 vols., Oxford, 1916), Vol. I.

Fowler, Henry Watson, and Francis George Fowler, translators. The Works of Lucian of Samosata. 4 vols. Oxford, 1905.

Fraunce, Abraham. The Arcadian Rhetorike. London, 1588.

Fuller, Thomas. The History of the Worthies of England. Edited by P. Austin Nuttall. 3 vols. London, 1840.

Fulwood, William. The Enimie of Idlenesse. London, 1568.

Gilbert, Sir Humphrey. Queene Elizabethes Achademy. Edited by Frederick J. Furnivall. London, 1869. Early English Text Society.

Gilbert, William. On the Loadstone and Magnetic Bodies. Translation of *De Magnete* by P. F. Mottelay. New York, 1893.

Greg, W. W., editor. Ben Jonson's *Sad Shepherd.* Louvain, 1905.

Guarino, Battista. De Ordine Docendi et Studendi. Translated by William H. Woodward in *Vittorino da Feltre and Other Humanist Educators.* Cambridge, England, 1897.

Hart, H. C. "Ben Jonson and Gabriel Harvey." *Notes and Queries,* 9th ser. XI (1903), 501–502.

Hazlitt, William. Lectures on the Dramatic Literature of the Age of Elizabeth. In *The Collected Works,* edited by A. R. Waller and Arnold Glover (13 vols., London and New York, 1902–6), Vol. V.

Henry, Aurelia, editor. Epicoene or The Silent Woman by Ben Jonson. New York, 1906. "Yale Studies in English," XXXI.

Herrick, Marvin T. "The Early History of Aristotle's *Rhetoric* in England." *Philological Quarterly,* V (1926), 242–57.

Hoole, Charles. A New Discovery of the Old Art of Teaching School. Edited by E. T. Campagnac. Liverpool, 1913.

Horace. Satires. Epistles. Ars Poetica. With an English translation by H. Rushton Fairclough. London, 1926. Loeb Classical Library.

Hoskyns, John. "Directions for Speech and Style." In *The Life, Letters, and Writings* by Louise Brown Osborn. New Haven, 1937. "Yale Studies in English," LXXXVII.

Hudson, Hoyt H. "Jewel's Oration against Rhetoric: a Translation." *Quarterly Journal of Speech*, XIV (1928), 374–92.

Hutchinson, F. E. "The English Pulpit from Fisher to Donne." In *Cambridge History of English Literature*, Vol. IV.

Irsay, Stephen d'. Histoire des universités. 2 vols. Paris, 1933–35.

Johnson, Ralph. The Scholar's Guide from the Accidence to the University. London, 1665.

Jonson, Ben. The Man and His Work. Edited by C. H. Herford, Percy and Evelyn Simpson. 10 vols. Oxford, 1925– .

—— Discoveries. Edited by Maurice Castelain. Paris, [1906].

—— The Poems. Edited by Bernard H. Newdigate. Oxford, 1936.

Jonsonus Virbius. London, 1638.

Knights, Lionel Charles. Drama and Society in the Age of Jonson. London, 1937.

Kyd, Thomas. Works. Edited by Frederick S. Boas. Oxford, 1901.

Lamb, Charles. Specimens of English Dramatic Poets. In *Works*, edited by William MacDonald (12 vols., London, 1903), Vol. VI.

Lever, Ralph. The Arte of Reason. London, 1573.

Levin, Harry. Ben Jonson Selected Works. New York, 1938.

Lucian. With an English translation by A. M. Harmon. 8 vols. London and New York, 1919– . Loeb Classical Library.

Lyly, John. Euphues: the Anatomy of Wit. Edited by Morris W. Croll and Harry Clemons. London, 1916.

—— Works. Edited by R. W. Bond. 3 vols. Oxford, 1902.

McGrew, J. F. "Bibliography of the Works on Speech Composition in England during the 16th and 17th Centuries." *Quarterly Journal of Speech*, XV (1929), 381–412.

Manly, John M. "Chaucer and the Rhetoricians." *Proceedings of the British Academy*, 1926.

Marlowe, Christopher. Tamburlaine the Great. Edited by U. M. Ellis-Fermor. London, 1930.

—— The Jew of Malta. In *The Jew of Malta and The Massacre at Paris*. Edited by H. S. Bennett. New York, 1931.

Marston, John. The Plays. Edited by H. Harvey Wood. 3 vols. Edinburgh and London, 1934–39.

—— The Scourge of Villanie. Edited by G. B. Harrison. London and New York, 1925.

Meridier, Louis. L'Influence de la seconde sophistique sur l'œuvre de Gregoire de Nysse. Paris, 1906.

Mulcaster, Richard. The Elementarie. Edited by E. T. Campagnac. Oxford, 1925.

[Munday, Anthony? translator]. Fidele and Fortunio, the Two Italian Gentlemen. Malone Society Reprints, 1909, Supplement, 1933.

Myrick, Kenneth Orne. Sir Philip Sidney as a Literary Craftsman. Cambridge, Mass., 1935.

Neumann, Joshua H. "Notes on Ben Jonson's English." *PMLA*, LIV (1939), 736–63.

Noyes, Robert Gale. Ben Jonson on the English Stage 1660–1776. Cambridge, Mass., 1935.

Owst, Gerald R. Preaching in Medieval England. Cambridge, England, 1926.

Padelford, Frederick Morgan. Select Translations from Scaliger's *Poetics*. New York, 1905. "Yale Studies in English," XXVI.

Paetow, Louis J. The Arts Course at Medieval Universities. Urbana, 1910. "University of Illinois, The University Studies," Vol. III, No. 7.

Peacham, Henry. The Garden of Eloquence. Revised edition. London, 1593.

Perry, Henry Ten Eyck. Masters of Dramatic Comedy. Cambridge, Mass., 1939.

Pettie, George, translator. The Civile Conversation of M. Steeven Guazzo. 2 vols. London and New York, 1925. The Tudor Translations.

Plato. Dialogues. Translated by B. Jowett. 2 vols. New York, 1937.

Puttenham, George. The Arte of English Poesie. Edited by Gladys Doidge Willcock and Alice Walker. Cambridge, England, 1936.

Quintilian. Institutio oratoria. With an English translation by H. E. Butler. 4 vols. London and New York, 1921–22. Loeb Classical Library.

Rainolde, Richard. A Booke Called The Foundacion of Rhetorike. London, 1563.

Rashdall, Hastings. The Universities of Europe in the Middle Ages. Edited by F. M. Powicke and A. B. Emden. 3 vols. Oxford, 1936.

Rea, John D., editor. Volpone, or The Fox by Ben Jonson. New Haven, 1919. "Yale Studies in English," LIX.

Sandford, William P. "English Rhetoric Reverts to Classicism 1600–1650." *Quarterly Journal of Speech*, XV (1929), 503–25.

Sandys, John Edwin. History of Classical Scholarship. 2d ed., 3 vols. Cambridge, England, 1906–8.

Sargeaunt, John. Annals of Westminster School. London, 1898.

Schelling, Felix E. Elizabethan Drama 1558–1642. 2 vols. Boston, 1908.

Schirmer, Walter. "Shakespeare und die Rhetorik." *Shakespeare-Jahrbuch*, LXXI (1935), 11–31.

Scot, Reginald. The Discoverie of Witchcraft. Edited by Brinsley Nicholson. London, 1886.

Scott, Izora. Controversies over the Imitation of Cicero. New York, 1910.

Sedgewick, G. G. Of Irony, Especially in Drama. Toronto, 1935.

Shakespeare. The Complete Works. Edited by George Lyman Kittredge. Boston, 1936.

Sherry, Richard. A Treatise of the Figures of Grammer and Rhetorike. London, 1555.

Silvayn, Alexander. The Orator. Translated by L. P. [Anthony Munday]. London, 1586.

Small, R. A. The Stage-Quarrel between Ben Jonson and the So-called Poetasters. Breslau, 1899.

Smith, G. Gregory. Ben Jonson. London, 1919.

—— Elizabethan Critical Essays. 2 vols. Oxford, 1904.

Spenser, Edmund. The Shepherd's Calendar. Edited by W. L. Renwick. London, 1930.

Spurgeon, Caroline. Shakespeare's Imagery. New York, 1936.

Stoll, Elmer Edgar. Poets and Playwrights. Minneapolis, 1930.

—— Shakespeare Studies. New York, 1927.

Symonds, John Addington. Ben Jonson. New York, 1886.

Tanner, Lawrence Edward. Westminster School: a History. London, 1934.

Thomson, James A. K. "Erasmus in England." In *England und die Antike*. Edited by Fritz Saxl. Leipzig and Berlin, 1932.

—— Irony. Cambridge, Mass., 1927.

Upton, James. Remarks on Three Plays of Benjamin Jonson. London, 1749.

Wagner, Russell A. "Wilson and His Sources." *Quarterly Journal of Speech*, XV (1929), 525–37.

Wallace, Karl R. "Bacon's Conception of Rhetoric." *Speech Monographs*, III (1936), 21–48.

—— Francis Bacon on Communication and Rhetoric. Chapel Hill, N.C., 1943.

Watson, Foster. English Grammar Schools to 1660. Cambridge, England, 1908.

Wheeler, Charles Francis. Classical Mythology in the Plays, Masques, and Poems of Ben Jonson. Princeton, 1938.

Willcock, Gladys Doidge. Shakespeare as a Critic of Language. London, 1934.

Williamson, George. "Senecan Style in the Seventeenth Century." *Philological Quarterly*, XV (1936), 321–51.

Wilson, Thomas. The Arte of Rhetorique. Edited by G. H. Mair. Oxford, 1909.

Woodward, William H. Studies in Education during the Age of the Renaissance. Cambridge, England, 1924.

Worcester, David. The Art of Satire. Cambridge, Mass., 1940.

INDEX